The Most Blessed People on Earth

Lonnie & Vicki Nelson

The Most Blessed People on Earth
© 2012 Lonnie and Vicki Nelson. All rights reserved.

All scripture is quoted from the Kings James Version of the Bible.

Published in the USA by:
Five Crowns Publishing
6246 Pettus Road
Antioch, TN 37013
www.JesusChristiscomingback.com

Library of Congress Control Number: 2012936048

Printed in the United States of America
ISBN 978-0-615-62053-4

Book design and layout by Darlene Swanson • www.van-garde.com

Contents:

Acknowledgements

The God and Father of our Lord and Savior Jesus Christ stands first and foremost in receiving our thankfulness, gratitude and worship for allowing us to learn His Word in regard to His blessings to His people.

We would also like to thank Samuel Nelson, Amber Nelson and Nelda Whynot for their love, support and help with this endeavor.

Introduction

From God's perspective, prosperity includes health, abundance, peace, joy, forgiveness and believing and trust toward God.

Throughout the history of God's Word, God's people are shown to be the most blessed people on earth. Men and women such as Hannah, Ruth, Mary, Lydia, Debra, David, Solomon, Zacchaesus, Joseph, Boaz, and Joshua, just to name a few, have had wealth, peace, fellowship with God and lived and enjoyed life to the fullest more than any other people on earth.

One of the greatest healing truths of God's Word is His forgiveness. Knowing and believing in your heart that you are completely forgiven by God relieves and alleviates guilt, condemnation, unworthiness and sin-consciousness. To be blessed by God is to have peace and fellowship with Him. All these things are part of God's prosperity.

The Most Blessed People On Earth will help you prosper in every category of life.

Chapter One

God's Image of You

God gave Jesus Christ many titles. He is called the Messiah, Savior, the Christ, the Sacrificial Lamb, Redeemer, Lord of Lords, King of Kings just to name a few. The relationship between God and man depended upon the accomplishments of Jesus Christ. Christ speaking the words "It is finished," while hanging on the cross was the catalyst that made becoming a son of God by birth possible. Fifty days later, on the day of Pentecost, people got born again as they were filled with the holy spirit and spoke in tongues for the first time. That is still God's primary will for his kids when they get born again. God has always wanted companionship. He wanted a family. He wanted children who would live with Him forever and that is why He planned our redemption through Jesus Christ. All of this was done so that you and I could be His children.

The only worthwhile estimation, portrait or picture of yourself to carry in your mind is God's image of you. No one holds a more esteemed image of you than God. It's far greater than any portrait you could mentally paint of yourself. God paints who we really are on the canvas of His word. We are His sons and daughters. Making us His children is the greatest thing God ever did for us. We are children of the Almighty God, the Creator of the heavens and the earth. We are sons and daughters of the God and Father of our Lord and Savior Jesus Christ. We have the highest title or position a man or woman could be exalted to. In God's eyes the kings, queens, princes, presidents, nobility or any other position, title or rank of this world do not even approach that of a son of the Most High God. It may not appear to the world what and who we are yet, but it is still the truth of God's Word. Although, we sometimes break fellowship with our Father, our standing before God is always one of being his son.

Being God's son entitles you to all the benefits and privileges that come with that name. God tells us all about our entitlements, advantages and birthrights in His Word. Nothing builds self-image, self-esteem and helps a person like the Word of God. It's the truth of God that makes a person free – free to live love. God's truth gives you mental peace and abundance. When God's Word is believed, we are healed in body, soul and mind. No therapist, psychiatrist, counselor or psychologist could help you like the help that you receive being a son of God who knows his Father. Let's look at the image God has of us though his eyes which we find in His Word.

I John 3:1 & 2

Behold, what manner of love the Father hath
bestowed upon us, that we should be called the
sons of God: therefore the world knoweth us
not, because it knew him not.

Beloved, now are we the sons of God, and it
doth not yet appear what we shall be: but we
know that, when he shall appear, we shall be like
him; for we shall see him as he is.

God has bestowed an unfathomable amount of love upon
us. However, the world will never recognize or give you any ac-
claim for who you are in God's eyes. Even though the greatest
part of who we are is yet to come, we are sons of God right now
and we can carry the mind picture of ourselves that God does.

Let's look at some of the wonderful things God does for His
people and some of the amazing promises God makes in His
Word that we can claim. Job was a believing man of God. Look
what God taught him.

Job 12:3

But I have understanding as well as you; I am
not inferior to you: yea, who knoweth not such
things as these?

Too many of us allow society to dictate to us who we are, where we can go and what we can do. You are not inferior to anyone else. You are not at the mercy of your environment. We do not have to accept the constrictive restraints that the world tries to place on us. We do not have to allow people to put us in a box. We are not lower or less important than anyone else. God's son is the best thing you will ever be. I often say you can't top what God has done for me. I am God's son and I have eternal life! Can you top or do better than that? We undervalue who God has made us to be, and overprice who the world says we are. With God all things are possible and you can accomplish anything according to God's Word.

Exodus 14:14

The LORD shall fight for you, and ye shall hold your peace.

Those people did not let others steal their peace. How can you lose with God fighting for you? No matter how big the monsters of your mind are, God is greater. He is the one that fights for you. Try this exercise. Imagine some fictitious being in your mind. Do your worst: you know claws, fangs, whatever powerful being you can dream up. Now imagine God, the Almighty Creator of the heavens, stars, universes and galaxies. That little "gremlin" that you made up in your mind is a pathetic, imaginary weakling compared to God! God is REAL!

I John 4:4

Ye are of God, little children, and have overcome
them: because greater is he that is in you, than
he that is in the world.

You have overcome the world and all the negatives in it. You
just have to claim it and live it. We have the spirit of God within
us. It's Christ in you. You have a lot of power in you.

Ephesians 1:19

And what is the exceeding greatness of his
power to us-ward who believe, according to the
working of his mighty power.

God did not throw this verse in His Word because He
thought, "Oh yeah, exceeding greatness, that sounds really
good." God put this promise in His word for His children to
read, believe and claim! It's in the unleashing of our believing
that we see the power of God. Take the muzzle off your believing. The people in God's Word manifested their believing with
signs, miracles and wonders. We are equipped to live that power
manifested today. We are His children.

Mark 9:23

Jesus said unto him, If thou canst believe, all
things are possible to him that believeth.

This is a promise and it is a truth that God has given us. The
principle of believing directs and determines your life more than
anything else. When fear in your soul tells you that you cannot
believe God, then believe God anyway and shut its mouth and
silence its voice. The only loss you could have in light of this
verse is just being afraid to live it.

What value does God put on you? With God, cost of item
equals value of item. It cost God His only begotten son to save
you and make you His son. That's the value we have to God. We
are eternally sons of God. God only made one of you. You are
so unique and beautiful in God's eyes that He wants only one of
you. Open your spiritual eyes and see yourself like God sees you.

Psalm 29:11

The LORD will give strength unto his people;
the LORD will bless his people with peace.

The Lord will give you strength for whatever you need. Paul
said he learned to be abased and to abound. Paul learned how to
be blessed and live whether he had little or much. And it's a great
lesson to learn in living. However, In light of all of the promises

in God's Word, little of our lives should be abased. We ought to be abounding so that our need is met and we have plenty to give. We don't have to succumb to poverty. Don't quit and just settle for the crumbs of the world. God makes winners! The adversary makes losers. What you manifest by your believing will determine your outcome.

God will absolutely give us strength. That's mental toughness. The people in the Word that did great things for God were mentally tough. It was the Word of God that gave them that mental strength to accomplish whatever needed to be done.

Psalm 147:3

He healeth the broken in heart, and bindeth up
their wounds.

God is the great healer of broken hearts. When your heart is broken, crushed and shattered in pieces, God said He will bind up that wound. God is the One you want mending and working on your heart. God takes care of people like no other. In believing we get our healing.

John 14:27

Peace I leave with you, my peace I give unto you:
not as the world giveth, give I unto you. Let not
your heart be troubled, neither let it be afraid.

The world talks of peace while continually arming itself for war. There is no peace in the world or inner peace without Jesus Christ, the Prince of peace. He alone can give peace. Living the peace that God gives us through Jesus Christ is how God imagines us to be. It God's picture of how our lives are to be. This is God's representation of us. This is God's visual impression of how we are to be on the inside. People should see our lives and think we are an emulation of this verse. This is not just God's concept of us, it is His will for our lives. God's Word is God's will for our lives.

Romans 5:1

Therefore being justified by faith, we have peace
with God through our Lord Jesus Christ:

God is at peace with us. God is not huffing and puffing at you. God is not snapping and barking at you. His wrath is not hot and kindled toward you! He's not yelling at you, telling you that you have to do better. The concept of God as a wrathful, vengeful God comes from the adversary. The devil seeks to destroy our relationship with God by painting Him as an unforgiving, contemptible god. In no way does this idea come from God. God is not finding fault with us or blaming us for our sin or short-comings. God loves us. He made us and He knew full well how we would be. Just changing your thinking about Who and how God is will change your life. Change your mental imagine of God to the loving, kind Father that He is and then change your mental image of yourself. We have entirely too many fearful thoughts of what others think of us. Love yourself and stop it. It's what God thinks of you that's matters.

Jeremiah 29:11

For I know the thoughts that I think toward you, saith the LORD, thoughts of peace, and not of evil, to give you an expected end.

God is love, not sometimes, all the time. It says in Corinthians that the love of God thinks no evil. That means that the love of God thinks no evil of God, yourself or others. God does not have ANY evil thoughts about you – ever, never. Now, that's someone I want to spend time with and be around. God's thoughts of us are of peace. The word "peace" is used 429 times in the King James Version. Do you think God wants us to have some? This word "peace" means: exempt from rage and conflict, harmony and concord with God and self. We have nothing to fear from our Father. God is the Author of peace and there is no other place it comes from. Peace is the absence of conflict in our souls.

God does not want us afraid, or fearful of Him. I just do not understand why people want us to think of God as Someone who makes us tremble in fear before Him. Our minds and hearts are to be peaceful and at rest. God has called us to peace and made us worthy of peace. The ultimate peace with God comes in our intimate relationship with Him. Those believers in the Word and the believers of today know that. With that fellowship with God comes the absence of inner strife – you are untroubled and undisturbed. Knowing you are forgiven brings great peace. We are disposed to peace. When you have peace you are free from alarm, agitation and dreadful emotions.

(A side note regarding men who lack peace . . . Some women claim men have a kind of menstrual period also. I'll let you in on a little secret. About a year ago some male doctors found out that it was true. Thank God it was male doctors and it got buried asunder. I hear there are some female doctors on the hunt for this fact. Keep praying men, God has kept it a secret thus far. You know a merry heart doeth good like a medicine!)

Back to the end of that wonderful verse. . . The words, "an expected end" is a figure of speech called *hendiadys* which is two words used, but one thing meant. It could be said, "an end which I have caused you to hope for." The Old Testament believers' hope was the first coming of the Messiah. Today, our greatest hope is eternal life with Christ's return. However, God also wants us to have hopes and dreams in this life. And, God wants those dreams fulfilled.

You will never find what you are looking for in this life until you open the door of God's Word. It's the only place you will find God's heart and blessing for your life. You won't find the "therapy" that God's Word gives you anywhere else.

The world is not a positive or uplifting place. Our culture and environment has had a negative effect on all of us. However, we do not have to be at the mercy of the world or held captive by what it thinks it sees in us. The world is perpetually trying to make you something you are not. You are what GOD SAYS YOU ARE! The most important viewpoint you can have of yourself is God's view. The devil's or other people's opinions of your life should surely not become yours. Of course, there are those who are truly helping you grow and you should heed their advice. The heart of this chapter is for you to see all that God has made you and wants for you by being His son. Nobody wants more for you than He does. He wants us to continue raising our level of expectation from Him. Look at what He did for all the people in His Word.

God has made us able to live the following verse. Are we willing?

Philippians 4:13

I can do all things through Christ which strengtheneth me.

We are who God says we are. We can do what God says we can do. What limits can you put on walking with God? We can expect miracles, wonders, and signs. God will never do less than

His Word, however He can go beyond it and do more. And when God does more than He promises it is call phenomena. Phenomena is when God decides to go above and beyond what He promises in His Word. If it's God's good pleasure to do that, hallelujah. There is tremendous power seen, when God decides to do that.

II Corinthians 2:14

Now thanks be unto God, which always causeth
us to triumph in Christ, and maketh manifest
the savour of his knowledge by us in every place.

We are to celebrate in triumph and thank God for it. God causes us to triumph in Christ. God leads us in triumph. We are to triumph over whatever is holding us back and too often that's our own selves. God will lead us in triumph.

I John 5:4

For whatsoever is born of God overcometh the
world: and this is the victory that overcometh
the world, even our faith [believing].

It's only by believing that people overcome. You have to root out the negatives in your mind and life with the truth of God's Word. This verse is twofold. The first part says that when we are born of God, we get eternal life. We are born again and we beat the world and are heaven bound and the world can't stop us from going. Secondly, we can also live the more abundant life now, right now. We overcome the negatives in the world by our believing.

John 8:32

And ye shall know the truth, and the truth shall make you free.

John 8:36

If the Son therefore shall make you free, ye shall be free indeed.

God has made us a free people. However, It's only the TRUTH of the Word of God that makes us free. It's a freedom in the heart and mind that only comes from God. The more of the truth we put on, the freer our lives become. It's a continual lifetime process. Our life and our walk with God just gets better all the time. We are free from the slavery and bondage of fear and torment. We are not under the control, restrained or confined in our hearts and souls by any one. We are free to pursue our own choices and our own dreams. We are free to be candid and open with God. Keep the tail of your heart always wagging with God and your soul purring in His presence.

The salvation of man is a free gift of grace. My soul still sins but my heart is free. We have freedom from pain and suffering. We are not encumbered or restricted by others. The Word rids, strips and clears the heart of all the garbage and trash that taints it.

Romans 8:32

He that spared not his own Son, but delivered
him up for us all, how shall he not with him also
freely give us all things?

God did not spare His son for us. If God could have spared or held back any thing for us that would have been it. God freely gives us all things. All things from God are as free as the air we breathe. Only God could make a promise of this magnitude.

Proverbs 28:1

The wicked flee when no man pursueth: but the
righteous are bold as a lion.

The lion in this verse is a lion in his prime. He is a symbol of power and courage. This Lion is extremely protective of his family. In his natural habitat, the lion is bold and travels without fear. No one can defeat him and he knows it. With freedom comes boldness. With that kind of boldness we can pursue our goals and dreams. We are to be bold in speaking God's Word and bold in living it. We have boldness before God's throne of grace. We are bold and fearless in just living life. Boldness in action overcomes more fear than can be enumerated. The image to carry of yourself is one that is fit for a king – King of the Serengeti.

Romans 8:37

> Nay, in all these things we are more than con-
> querors through him that loved us.

It does not say "conquerors." It says more than conquerors. As sons of God, this is who we truly are. We are sons who have victory beyond measure. With all that God has done for us, how could you be any less than more than a conqueror?

Titus 1:2

> In hope of eternal life, which God, that cannot
> lie, promised before the world began;

God cannot lie. We can be very thankful for the things God can't do as well as the things He can do. God will always, always be honest with us. And God promised us eternal life with Him forever. What image of yourself could you value more than one of living with God for eternity?

SPIRITUAL GOODIES For God's Image of You

- When you look for love from God you will never be rejected or disappointed in your expectations.

- Spirit is thicker than blood. It's a greater truth that my earthly son is my brother in Christ, and God is our Father, than I am his father and he is my son. If neither one of us were born again, we could not love each other with the love of God. We could only love with human love, which is far less. This is also true in marriage.

- To see and experience God's love requires believing.

- I want to be dependent upon God only.

- Of all the things we make time for in life, don't allow this one to elude you. Take time often and let God know you love Him. It's the one thing He always gets too little of.

- God help my wife carry an image of me and treat me like my dog does.

- God makes life meaningful. Without God what could possibly be the meaning of life? Life would have no point at all. We would just live and die forever. Without God how could life be more miserable?

- There is no one that is not needful or useful in the body of Christ. That's God's take on it, but it's not always mans.

- God's Word enables you to overcome fears that have stopped you before.

- The future is as bright as the promises of God. You could not have a brighter future painted for you than the one in God's Word.

- If you have a fear, forsake it or that fear may hamper you.

- Imagine God wants us to come live with Him in His home forever and ever. He's the only one to ever ask. Who else could offer that?

- This is just my life with God and how I live it. When I'm going about my daily life, out and about, I'm confident that God will always let me know if something bad is about to happen. If you knew something was going to happen to your child you would tell them. God loves us far more than we do our kids. I have weaknesses in my life but I also have strengths with God. I am very thankful for learning from Him through His Word. That still small voice has saved my life many times over. God is more willing to give us revelation than we realize. We just need to listen with our spiritual ears.

- The greatest power ever given by God came on the day of Pentecost. Man received God's spirit, His seed, that day and we have that seed in us today. God, Who is Spirit, speaks to His creation in you which is now your spirit, and that spirit which is Christ in you, communicates to your mind and heart. The still, small voice is just the tip of the iceberg in God's variety of ways that He communicates with His people.

- God has a sweet craving for fellowship with you.

- Too many of God's people are sin-conscious and equate poverty with self-righteousness.

- Tell the adversary to kiss your glass.

- The three greatest principals in life bar none are faith, hope and charity.

I Corinthians 13:13

And now abideth faith [believing], hope, charity [love], these three; but the greatest of these is charity.

Hebrews 12:2

Looking unto Jesus the author and finisher of
our faith; who for the joy that was set before him
endured the cross, despising the shame, and is
set down at the right hand of the throne of God.

- The joy set before him is at the end of the verse. You could not be given a greater hope or honor, than to sit on the right hand of the throne of God. The joy of that hope would aspire. Then also to be the Savior of the world, I have no words for that.

- Believe and act like it is impossible to fail.

- You can have and do anything you want, you just have to give up the belief that you can't.

- Feelings don't have to be a bad thing. God gave them to all of us. Do your best to think good thoughts, the thoughts of God's Word, and good feelings will follow. God gave us feelings and I feel good about it, and it feels great. When you love God and His people it feels good and that's the way God made us to be. It is the scale of God's Word with which we are to weigh all things.

- Don't let your day end full of wrath and rage. Do all you can to end anger that day so that your wrath does not "snowball." And by the way, you will sleep better.

Ephesians 4:26

Be ye angry, and sin not: let not the sun go
down upon your wrath.

- You get to know God by believing.

- God is more willing than we know to help us overcome.

- You will never find happiness in and of yourself.

- We undervalue what God has made us and overvalue the price the world puts on us.

- When you know God thinks only good about you, you can think good of yourself and others will join in.

- You will not find a better image of yourself than God's image of you.

- You will never find what you are looking for until you open the door of God's Word.

- God bless you with the level of your cup, I thank God mine is running over. It's the windows of heaven open and God pouring out a blessing.

- We have Christ in us, however we have to renew our minds to manifest his likeness on the outside so that we can enjoy him more on the inside.

- We are God's dwelling place. Remember. God would not live in some old, condemned home or building. He chose you, a living tabernacle.

- God's spiritual nature in you is your eternal life.

- With God, you will never have to look over your shoulder.

- It's amazing how many problems people have that exist only in their imagination.

- The devil brings all the fear of the improbable.

- God always does the right thing and sometimes that's to humor you and make you laugh.

- God's love is perfect. When you know you are loved by Him, you realize no one is loved more than you.

- Nothing will build more self-worth in your soul than knowing how worthy God has made you.

- I am not sure what God gives away more of, His forgiveness or His love. It will only be His love in the next life. Glory hallelujah.

- Only God knows how many people live alone in their heart.

- The love of God you have on the inside needs to be continually watered and nurtured by the word of God.

- It may appear that the leaders in the body of Christ sin less, however, they really just pick themselves up quicker.

Chapter Two

Honoring the Lord

One of the great principles to receiving prosperity from God is to give God honor. Ascertaining how to honor the Lord is a wonderful adventure into God's Word. To search out and find God's heart and thoughts on the subject of prosperity is an amazing journey. We want to find God's ideas and perspective on how to best handle our income and live our lives with a healthy body. We are to give honor where honor is due.

Proverbs 3:9 – 10

vs 9   Honour the LORD with thy substance,
and with the firstfruits of all thine increase:

vs 10   So shall thy barns be filled with plenty,
and thy presses shall burst out with new wine.

The Hebrew word for "honour" is the word *kabed* which means to glorify, weighty, to regard worthy of honour, to promote to honour. God is completely worthy of the honor we give

Him. No one or no thing is equal to or more worthy of our honor than God. When it comes to giving honor to God, it ought to hold first place in our heart.

We give God the honor His name is due when we give to the outreach of God's Word and to help God's people. To honor God is to give God the esteem HE is due with our income. We give because God is worthy of our love and respect. Giving is an expression in our thoughts and actions that God is worthy of our honor. And only God has this distinction and is exalted to this position with this honor. He is first in our finances. He is second to none. Too many other things are first for most people. People like Solomon, Ruth, Hannah, Job, Malachi, and the names go on, they knew where everything came from, who made everything. And in their tithing, God was exalted. These people knew what was really going on in life, and they gave God glory because they loved Him and they understood where the blessings in life come from, God.

God's people need to recover the knowledge of living and doing God's Word regarding giving and receiving in their finances and resources. There is no substitute, nor could you put anything else in the place of that which gives this honor. There is nothing else we can do in our walks to fulfill the honor of this purpose. It's like prayer, what could you substitute for it or what could you put in place of it? Prayer stands alone. It is a unique relationship that a Christian has with God. Is praying more important than giving and receiving, and sowing and reaping? I have not seen or read that anywhere in God's Word. Likewise, giving and receiving is also a unique relationship that a believer has with God. Giving and receiving is the main key of prosperity and health for God's people in His Word.

Too often money carries a value in a man's heart that is tainted. If we have a love and an over desire for wealth, that's a bad root to let grow. Money, wealth, materials things, power and many other things can become a person's god. However we do not want to be poor. Only God's Word can put that fire out in the heart and life of a man. Operating the principle of giving and receiving is the best ingredient I know to keep a heart in check. You're going to have a god in your life; you just have to make up in your mind which god it's going to be. Some people have one, some have many. Some of my motive in giving is to help me not be or become what I don't want to be. Sowing and reaping allows you to own your possessions, instead of your belongings owning you. When you give back to God, you proclaim by your actions that He is your God, not wealth and material things.

Our substance is our money and wealth, what God has blessed you with. And, what is important here is that we give with love in our hearts and the proper devotion in our souls, because we want to. You decide what work of God you want to support financially. It is your choice and decision what organization, church, ministry or charity that is moving God's Word that you want to give to. But wherever that may be, we are to give of our first fruits, not second, or somewhere else down the line. The word "firstfruits" means: first in progression and time in our hearts; that it precedes all others in our heart and time. If you can learn to keep God first here, you won't have nearly the trouble you might have had in other areas of your life. Giving is a wonderful key to a healthy life, especially when we give it to God. Wherever I sow my seed, in my heart I say, "This is for you God to help your people." After all, I am only giving back to God what is His. King David understood where everything came from. I Chronicles records David's heart.

I Chronicles 29:14

But who am I, and what is my people, that we
should be able to offer so willingly after this
sort? for all things come of thee, and of thine
own have we given thee.

This is the kind of heart God loves and is looking for.

Psalm 89:11

The heavens are thine, the earth also is thine: as
for the world and the fulness thereof, thou hast
founded them.

In our giving and receiving to God first, we are showing and giving reverence and submission to what He says in His Word. It's God's way of making it possible to pay our respect and our regard to God for all He does for us. To give a portion faithfully and consistently of our income is that which honors God. When we start giving and receiving, we are restoring to God the honorary glory He has earned and deserves. Don't allow God to be destitute of this honor in your life. It is an honor to serve God in this way.

All that is in the earth is God's. The living planet called Earth that is sustained by all living things; that provides water, food, and shelter, was created by God and belongs to Him alone. We are simply enjoying the benefits of what He placed in the earth for us to reap. From simple foods such as vegetables and fruit, crops and herds and materials such as linens, cottons and silks, to the diamonds and gold of the mines of the earth, we have received it all from Him. When we give back to God of our first-fruits, we are simply sowing a seed to reap another benefit from Him. It is in His nature to love people and give to people. When we give and receive with the love of God in our hearts, we imitate the heart of God. God made us to be loved by Him and to love Him back. Are you thankful God made you? The closer you get with God the more thankful you will be. Your thankfulness would bless no one more than God Himself.

Proverbs 14:31

He that oppresseth the poor reproacheth his
Maker: but he that honoureth [*kabed*] him hath
mercy on the poor [humble].

When we give of our substance, we send it forth with prayer and thanksgiving that it will bless all the people and all the places that it will reach and touch. We give with believing for the outreach of God's Word. In the body of Christ, which is the family of God, anyone can apply the principle of giving and receiving. The blessings and benefits are available to anyone. When you withhold the honor of giving back to God, you hurt yourself by stopping the blessing that you would have received. The act of giving is not just monetary. You give whatever you have: love, encouragement, kindness, money, time. That is exalting God with honor. Who holds more of a reputable position than God? Let's recognize and hold God with honor in our hearts. God has made it where you have the privilege to "do the honors."

If we know just a little about God, we realize that God has that which attracts honor, rather than honor that is just given; it is honor that is earned. The people in the Word that loved God, gave God the recognition of His worth. He was worth more to them than anything else in the world. Who or what is more important in your life than God? One of the characteristics of this word honor is to give God importance. I trust you can see the heart behind this. Only God has the key to a woman or man's heart. Only God truly knows your heart. Not only is God honored when we faithfully practice the giving of our firstfruits, He also honors His Word in keeping to His promise, knowing He will cultivate this kind of heart in a person.

Acts 20:35

> I have shewed you all things, how that so labouring ye ought to support the weak, and to remember the words of the Lord Jesus, how he said, It is more blessed to give than to receive.

God wants people to know this truth and live it. As you give you receive. People have because they give. Giving allows you to receive so that you have more to give.

There are times when receiving comes close to rivaling giving, however, when we get to be on the giving side, it is a huge joy in the heart. Sometimes, when I'm out having lunch, I see people bowing their heads in prayer for the food God has blessed them with. Sometimes they hold hands. Sometimes they pray out loud and other times they are silent in prayer. Now and then I've called over their server and asked to have their bill with instructions to tell them, "God bless." They rarely know who paid for their lunch. However, some just have to know who paid for their meal and they find me before I have a chance to get to my vehicle. In either case, they give God the glory. There is a joy in that giving, that is so sweet nothing else is quite like it – the simple joy of giving for no other purpose than to give and bless.

I don't need to tell you it can be a blessing to receive also. Most people have no problem with receiving. Giving is the part that we need to learn. We are to be a part of helping those less fortunate Christians. It is a greater blessing to give than to receive. When you start giving, insurmountable challenges will become minor obstacles. There is a law working here. In order to give, you have had to receive. God will give back to you when you give.

The believers in the book of Philippians believed in the principle and lived it. Later, other Christians helped Paul financially as well. We all should give to those who are teaching and helping us with God's Word. Men and women who see to the needs of God's people and help them live the more abundant life, should receive financially from those whom they help. It is not only the right thing to do, it is the will of God to give to those who are watching over God's household.

Philippians 4:15

Now ye Philippians know also, that in the
beginning of the gospel, when I departed from
Macedonia, no church communicated [shared
financially] with me as concerning giving and
receiving, but ye only.

The phrase giving and receiving is very unique and important. Those in the family of God, who believe in giving and receiving, know that the principle and the promise works. In the church, we all know some of these people. They seem to spread their wings in abundance and fly away. In order to produce results, we must apply the principle. Just wishing for things to change in your life or hoping things will get better will just keep everything the same, usually things get worse.

I have heard many Christian people say that they are "believing" God. How often have we thought about the word "believing?" Just like we learned in elementary school, putting an "ing" on the end of a word makes it a verb. Verbs are "doing" words. They are "action" words. Believing is a verb and a verb connotes action. Believing in action is not sitting around just waiting for results. If you want to eat, do you sit in your living room and wait for a meal to drop in your lap from heaven? (Or, maybe from your wife or husband). Usually, you have to get up and go make yourself something to eat. Life is full of principles and taking believing action is one of them. When we sow seed and/or give, we are taking believing action. We believe with our actions that God's Word is true and His promises are real.

Those who take God at His Word will live His Word, according to this promise.

Psalm 37:25

I have been young, and now am old; yet have
I not seen the righteous forsaken, nor his seed
begging bread.

The righteous are those who believe. God does not forsake them nor do His children need to beg for food. Operating the principle of giving and receiving is a great way of stopping life from just happening to you. Being committed in giving to God, is a huge way of building your believing. It builds your believing in a way that no other principle in God's Word does.

There is an innate thing in man for him to provide for his family. Even animals take care of their young. Of all the physical and material things there are in life, money perhaps holds more value to man than anything else. It means a great deal to mankind. It takes money to feed your family and to live in your home. It takes money to put clothes on your back and have and maintain a vehicle. Money is the most physical thing we use to acquire the physical things we need. It's one of the last things we would be willing to do without in the physical realm. With too many people, it's right on the heels of air, water and food. This is why God wants to reach our hearts in this area. It's important to God for us to give back to Him because of the vital role it plays in our lives. God's love and giving are without comparison.

In the Old Testament, God had them give of their cattle,

sheep, crops and many other things, because of the value and importance it carried in their hearts. God made us; He knows what we value. God could have used anything in terms of us giving back to Him. It could have been dirt. But then man still would have had the same problem. At first he would say, "Oh yeah I can give my dirt." Then the man starts to think about it and says, "Oh great does it have to be my top soil? You're not taking dirt from my property and carting it off somewhere else." If it was trash we would gladly give it and it would not mean a thing to us. Hmm, maybe not.

Isaiah 58:13

If thou turn away thy foot from the sabbath,
from doing thy pleasure on my holy day; and
call the sabbath a delight, the holy of the LORD,
honourable; and shalt honour him, not doing
thine own ways, nor finding thine own pleasure,
nor speaking thine own words:

Do you want to live like this? THINE own ways? THINE own pleasure? THINE own words? Not me. If you do, ask God to help you change. If not, thank God you never will. When it comes to truth, God holds nothing back. If our hearts are like this, God is going to let us know. If our hearts are pure (not perfect – that won't happen until Christ returns) when we give to

God, it is an honorable motive. Giving produces happiness by its own qualities and operation. It gives you a way of thinking something good about yourself. The principle of giving and receiving to God through His church does more for our self-image than we are aware of. It brings thoughts of self that will bless you before God and God will work within you so you can carry the image in your heart as a son or daughter of God. It does your heart good to give back to God.

God loves you no less or more if you give or don't give. You see, giving and receiving is not God's attitude toward you. Giving and receiving, sowing and reaping, is OUR ATTITUDE toward God. In our hearts God should hold our most exalted thoughts.

In the Old Testament believers were required to tithe and make offerings. They had to make their own atonements for their sins.

Exodus 30:15

The rich shall not give more, and the poor shall
not give less than half a shekel, when *they* give an
offering unto the Lord, to make an atonement for
your souls.

We are not required by the law to give. Jesus Christ fulfilled all the law including the tithe. I am so, so thankful that we don't have to keep the law. Jesus Christ was the offering and atonement for our souls. It's already been done!

So then, operating the principle of giving and receiving is God's way of endeavoring to help His people live and enjoy life. He does not want us living in fear, poverty, sickness or any kind of misery. So, He made this law to benefit His Old Testament people. It is important to note here that God never wanted to make laws for His people. It was not His idea. He wanted them to believe Him and trust Him, but they wanted rules and regulations to follow. Therefore, God laid out in His Word the laws that they would keep and do of which giving is one. Those who give with believing know the freedom and liberty it brings.

We must do the will of God, if we want the blessing of God. It's a spiritual principle. Spiritually it's the most fundamental key to material prosperity. God shows no favoritism and there is no respect of persons with Him. However, God does respect and honor the principles we operate. We give in recognition of the good God has given.

Exodus 35:21 & 22, 29

vs 21   And they came, every one whose heart stirred him up, and every one whom his spirit made willing, *and* they brought the Lord's offering to the work of the tabernacle of the congregation, and for all his service, and for the holy garments.

vs 22   And they came, both men and women, as many as were willing hearted, *and* brought bracelets, and earrings, and rings, and tablets, all jewels of gold: and every man that offered *offered* an offering of gold unto the Lord.

vs 29   The children of Israel brought a willing offering unto the Lord, every man and woman, whose heart made them willing to bring for all manner of work, which the Lord had command-ed to be made by the hand of Moses.

Who was the offering for and to? God. These people knew the reason they could give like this was because they understood the principle of giving and receiving. They lived the principle. They gave willingly; no one was twisting their arms or coercing them to give. They were giving in service to God for God's people.

Revelation 4:11

Thou art worthy, O Lord to receive glory and honour and power: for thou hast created all things, and for thy pleasure they are and were created.

God's will is never for us to be in debt up to our necks, not even our ankles. Who wants to be on the financial treadmill of poverty and defeat? All areas of our lives are to be blessed. The Word says the poor you will have with you always, but you don't have to be one of them. I wonder how often that has to do with the rich seeing to it. Remember the world will always try to keep you down, but God is the God of deliverance in all categories including the financial realm.

Prosperity doesn't just happen, at least for most of us, nor does poverty. If you were born into poverty, you don't have to continue to live in it. The biggest key in my life to prospering is honoring God first. It strengthens my believing to prosper and maintain my health more than any other principle I live. Giving and RECEIVING is a law which everyone can learn and apply.

In its least common denominator, it is fear that ruins a person. Fear is not going to defeat me, or cause me to be poor or sickly. Most Christians ignore and neglect God's Word on the subject of giving and receiving. They push aside the fact that it is God who is asking them to give. In fact, it usually gets put off for a person's whole life. They go a whole life time and never see God's heart or His purpose in why He wants us to give. The blessing is for you. God was just as blessed and living before we got here. He sure had a lot less problems before we got here. Uh, He's knows what He is doing. God loves us in spite of our shortcomings. I don't know how much on account of. There is a new day dawning when we will meet God and this life will all change. God says in His Word, if you believe in Jesus Christ and that God raised him from the dead, you will be saved. If you want the blessing, you believe the promise — the blessing of eternal life. The blessing of eternal life. If you don't believe, you don't receive. Only God sets the requirement on how eternal life will be obtained and received. He is the Author of eternal life. I don't know how God could have made it more simple. What could be more simple and easy than believing and receiving? You don't even have to move. Well maybe a few brain cells.

When we give of our firstfruits on a consistent basis, we are pledging our honor to God. In the material realm, it is the highest form of honor we can give God. When we live giving and receiving, we are conferring honor to God. Nothing or no one should be exalted more in our finances than God Himself. Only God has earned the title Honorable and only He should be exalted to the position of glory by our giving. God is to carry the highest veneration in our finances. We are to give God the distinction and notice for all He has done for us. Let's give God credit first for all we have. Nothing beats first place. God receives the blue ribbon in our finances. It's a wonderful blessing and reward to honor God with our firstfruits. Furthermore, the eternal blessings will be the best. If we could just get a glimpse of one eternal reward, we would be faithful for life.

Malachi 1:6

A son honoureth his father, and a servant his
master: if then I be a father, where is mine
honour? and if I be a master, where is my fear
[respect]? saith the LORD of hosts unto you,
O priests, that despise my name. And ye say,
Wherein have we despised thy name?

Remembering that the context of the Book of Malachi is
tithing, God is asking a question. If God is our Father and we are
His sons, where is His honor. I guess it's how much we believe
in the blessings that come from honoring God. Do you really
believe you will receive back? Our actions will be a good judge
of that. Our heavenly Father is to be first, in our money, and in
the material realm. God first place. Do we deem God worthy
of honor in our lives? Why would we want to put anything else
ahead of God when it comes to money?

Jeremiah 33:9

And it shall be to me a name of joy, a praise and an
honour before all the nations of the earth, which
shall hear all the good that I do unto them: and
they shall fear and tremble for all the goodness
and for all the prosperity that I procure unto it.

Not only do we receive blessings from giving to God, but in giving honor to God, we are called honorable by Him. It is by God's goodness that He prospers us. It is a great witness to each other and the world how God blesses His people. When people see how God has blessed you, they will say, "I want to prosper! I want to prosper and be an example too!" Who wouldn't?

Isaiah 43:4

Since thou wast precious in my sight, thou hast
been honourable, and I have loved thee: therefore
will I give men for thee, and people for thy life.

Israel did many other things before God in their walks that made them honorable. However, if His people did not tithe, God would not have called them honorable. Isaiah would not have been honourable if he did not tithe. In this section of God's Word, God called Israel honorable. God also used the word "since," which indicates time. From the time Israel tithed in this section they became honorable, which made them precious in God's sight. The Hebrew word "precious" is the word *yaqar* which means: be highly valuable, be prized, be costly. It's how we should want to be seen in God's sight. These are some of the blessings and benefits in giving a portion of our income to God.

Remember there is no consequences, curse or any of God's wrath whatsoever if we fail to give. God loves all of us. He forgives us all our sins and transgressions. However, you will not receive the blessings you would have if you withhold your giving to God.

Isaiah 43:23 – 25

vs 23   Thou hast not brought me the small cattle of thy burnt offerings; neither hast thou honoured me with thy sacrifices. I have not caused thee to serve with an offering, nor wearied thee with incense.

vs 24   Thou hast bought me no sweet cane with money, neither hast thou filled me with the fat of thy sacrifices: but thou hast made me to serve with thy sins, thou hast wearied me with thine iniquities.

vs 25   I, even I, am he that blotteth out thy transgressions for mine own sake, and will not remember thy sins.

What a heart of love God has for His people – His unconditional love. He is relentless in all His mercy and the forgiveness of our souls. Have you noticed that when we forgive, we often do it for our own sakes? God not only forgives us for Christ's sake and our sake, He forgives us for His own sake. God does not want to carry around in His heart and thoughts the load of all our past sins and weaknesses.

God's Word does tell us of the great benefits in giving.

Luke 6:38a

Give, and it shall be given unto you; good measure, pressed down, and shaken together, and running over, shall men give into your bosom.

What you value most you will honor first. Look at where a man spends his money, and you will know what his priorities are, what he values, and what is first in his life. Whenever we give to God we are conferring honor to Him, the honor He is worthy of for all the good He has done us. We know in our hearts He will continue to bless us and take care of us. What you honor and esteem most is where your money will be spent first. If you want the blessing, fulfill the promise. If you want God's best, give your best, and that would be giving to God first. If you don't need it or want it then don't give. God bless ya, and we will pray for you. And God loves you just as much as He loves Jesus Christ. Love gets no bigger than that.

Psalm 9:10

And they that know thy name will put their trust
in thee: for thou, LORD, hast not forsaken them
that seek thee.

Ecclesiastes 6:2a

A man to whom God hath given riches, wealth,
and honour, so that he wanteth nothing for his
soul of all that he desireth.

God Himself is the best place for riches, wealth and honor
to come from. He brings the greatest joy and satisfaction to your
life. There is no better key in bringing this to pass than honoring
God in our giving and receiving.

Does your giving and receiving to God of your income mean
anything to you ? Is your sowing and reaping significant to you?
Or is it just something you hardly ever do? If it doesn't mean
anything to God, then why does He have so much in His Word
about it? God doesn't need one material thing that we have. God
wants our love and trust in Him. God can be the best friend
you'll ever have. If Moses were here, he would tell you so. The
more faithful we are to give to God, the more we will grow to
trust and believe Him. God promises your life will be a lot better
off when you operate this principle. One of the most fundamental keys in learning to love God is in giving and receiving and in

our sowing and reaping. Operating this principle is a trust issue with God. Those who don't give will never have the bond and fellowship that this principle affords and offers.

Proverbs 8:17 & 18; 21

vs 17   I love them that love me; and those that seek me early shall find me.

vs 18   Riches and honour are with me; yea, durable riches and righteousness.

vs 21   That I may cause those that love me to inherit substance; and I will fill their treasures.

Those who have practiced the giving and receiving principle for a period of time know the importance it carries in God's heart. People like Moses, Malachi, Zacchaeus, Ruth and Mary, knew the principle and lived it. God will cause it to happen in your heart as you sow. It takes the pressure off the cooker in your heart and mind. God says He will fill their treasures. God will do His part, we must do our part. God will make sure we have everything we need. The word "fill" means to be abundant and over flowing. Our treasure will be abundant and overflowing. God has earned and deserves our honor. The very air we breathe comes from God.

The sowing of our seed includes giving to Christians who have genuine need.

I Corinthians 16:1 – 3

vs 1   Now concerning the collection for the
saints, as I have given order to the churches of
Galatia, even so do ye.

The word "saints" in the phrase "the collection for the saints"
is plural. The collection is for the body of Christ, the family of
God. That means people like you and me, if we have a genuine
need. This is God's order.

vs 2   Upon the first day of the week let every one
of you lay by him in store, as God hath prospered
him, that there be no gatherings when I come.

By doing the first verse you can live the second verse, as God
prospers you. God does His part because you lived your part.
We want God to do the prospering.

vs 3   And when I come, whomsoever ye
shall approve by your letters, them will I send
to bring your liberality [a gift of grace, benefit,
bounty] unto Jerusalem.

The "whomsoever ye shall approve" were approved couri-
ers, those trusted, would bring the liberality to Jerusalem. The
money did not just go to pay the bills. Now that is part of it,
however God's people, His saints, are to be helped as well. I

know I get blessed when I see and hear of people being helped. That's not the people you teach a life time to fish and they never learn. It's believers who are faithful and have proven themselves. Those ministers, who do give, know how much it means to the fellowship of their people. And, now and then, those who genuinely need help will be so blessed to receive it. God's people love to be around where God's family is loved and taken care of. Give and you will learn to really live. Apply the principle of giving and receiving now, because if Christ tarries it will be too late when others read your tombstone.

I have found that my life is a lot greater and more blessed in living this principle than when I did not live it. I thank God that I no longer have the fears and needs in my life that I once had. Because the devil is not dead, sometimes needs and fears try to creep up, but I maintain my peace, joy and believing. We may stagger some at the promises of God, but that does not mean failure.

Allow God to receive and enjoy the honor only we can give with hearts of love and respect for Him for all He has done and even more so for what He will continue to do for us. The greatest life that could ever be lived is the more abundant life that our brother, Jesus Christ, made available. The greatest blessings are yet to come.

SPIRITUAL GOODIES For Honoring the Lord

- Tell me it's not true. If you took a Gallop poll of Christians, you would find that they gave more in tips last year than they did to God. There must be something wrong with our scale of values. Why would some Christians wonder why they are poor materially or spiritually?

- "I never will not love," is a thought that may elude us, but it never did Christ.

- Giving of thanks is one of the biggest indicators of believing there is.

- Most of our limitations are self-induced and the devil is always willing to accommodate us.

- I will not be a slave to the material realm or any other earthly thing, and that includes people.

- The best attitude to have in financial giving is, "I am going to stay faithful to giving until Christ comes back or I die."

- Don't give God the back seat in your finances.

- We need to believe God to receive after we have given.

- It feels good to have some money in your pocket, just don't carry it in your heart.

- You set the standard for your receiving by your giving.

- To not have financial fear is how God wants us to live. And that's how I am going to live and be. Glory hallelujah!

- Don't allow prosperity and health to forsake you.

- The love of money will rack and ruin you. You can never get enough of something that you love. It's the love of money that so taints a person's heart. The love of it is the root of all evil, not the money itself. That root will effect and destroy the whole tree and it starts dying from the inside out.

- Sow and reap. Man don't "save" your wife from a life of prosperity.

- God, through His word, has done more for me than I will ever do for Him.

- After the Old Testament, tithing is not commanded nor is it rescinded.

Mark 12:17

And Jesus answering said unto them, Render to Caesar the things that are Caesar's, and to God the things that are God's. And they marvelled at him.

- There is a portion of our substance that belongs to God, but because we live in the day of grace God has left it entirely up to you what you do with it. You know, the thing that is truly God's should be our love for Him.

- Why are people offended and get angry when others don't leave a tip or leave a small one? And yet, when it comes time to give to God and they see others give nothing, they think nothing of it. That is backwards. No wonder people often have needs in their lives. It's time for a spiritual check-up. Who loves you more or can take better care of you than God?

- Selfishness is a quick way to sickness. So don't share, just eat all the candy.

- A street person told me the other day that they were on a money diet.

- The laborer is worthy of his hire. When I get paid, the portion of my money that I enjoy giving the most is the portion I give to God first. When I was a kid the two places I enjoyed spending my money the most was candy and toys. They've only been removed to second place so far.

- When you have arrived in faithfully giving of your finances to God first, not second or third, you have helped yourself in more areas of your life than you will ever know. However, what you reap in this life is just a drop in the ocean in comparison to what you will receive in the next life to live with for all eternity.

- Thank God often for a thankful heart.

- I give because I don't want to be poor.

- God deserves and has earned the honor of giving to Him first, more than any other place in our life.

- We are God's sons. Does He have anyone closer whom He would rather give to.

- Who could you possibly be more indebted to than God?

- Let thanks be given to God on account of and in spite of. Let giving be done in the same fashion.

- Who among us could ever earn a drop of God's love?

- Focus on giving thanks with gratefulness in your heart, then you're whining, whimpering and complaining will wane.

- What you sow you reap. If you want love give love.

- Thank God the King James Version of the Bible is not copyrighted. Because it isn't, it can be quoted, copied and printed by anyone. God holds the true "copyright" to His Word. If a group, ministry or denomination develops a new version of the Bible, if it is truly God's Word, why would they copyright it? If someone tries to copyright the King James Version, they need to be stopped. Only man would try to copyright the truth of God's Word. Books are one thing, but the Bible is another. If there was no King James Version and no group would give us permission to use "their" Bible, what would we do? How could we quote God's Word in this book? The first century Christians made copies of the gospels and epistles as they circulated from city to city.

Chapter Three

God Sent His Word and Healed Them

Y ou have probably heard some people say that God gave them a certain health condition or sickness, however, that is never written in God's Word. In fact, as you can see in the following verse, God's Word says the complete opposite!

III John 2

Beloved, I wish above all things that thou mayest prosper and be in health, even as thy soul prospereth.

John wrote this incredible promise, but it is God doing the speaking. The Greek word for the word "beloved" is the word *agapetos* which means: dearly loved, well-loved or loved ones. God calls us His beloved. When you love someone you only want the best for them. Why would God ever want us to suffer? He doesn't! In fact, the verse states, "I wish ABOVE ALL THINGS that thou may prosper and be in health."

Prosperity and health are so vital in our fellowship with God. Most Christians would agree, that the two most spiritually disabling things in our walk are financial troubles and sickness. These two ailments put so many people on the "spiritually unable to perform list." It is absolutely clear from this verse that it is the absolute will of God that we prosper and be in health. However, the main focus of this chapter is our physical health. God does not want us spiritually or physically crippled. It's too defeating in our Christian walk.

I thank God I'm rarely sick and when I am, I thank God for a quick recovery. However, when we are sick, lying flat on our back, we're stalled-out in being a witness; an ambassador for Christ. God wishes on no one to be bed ridden, ill or live with a disease. He desires that none of us require sick leave in our walks. However, being human, just about all of us have been sick or laid up for a while. I don't like being around anyone when I'm sick, mostly myself. Likewise, no one usually likes being around people who are broke either. Both conditions can often be followed by complaining and complaining has never helped anyone out of a negative situation whether it be bad health or poor finances. We have all been in similar negative situations, but we don't have to stay there. Sometimes we don't feel good but we keep keeping on. Then we get sick and we need to rest and take time to allow our bodies to heal. We can thank God He made our bodies to heal themselves. Sickness, poverty and death come from the devil not God.

Hebrews 2:14

Forasmuch then as the children are partakers of flesh and blood, he also himself [Jesus Christ] likewise took part of the same; that through death he might destroy him that had the power of death, that is, the devil.

John 10:10

The thief [the devil] cometh not, but for to steal, and to kill, and to destroy: I [Jesus Christ] am come that they might have life, and that they might have *it* more abundantly.

The adversary holds the power of death. The devil comes to steal, kill and destroy. The devil's will for mankind is sickness, poverty and death. He wants bondage and mental shackles for the Christian.

God wants us blessed, happy, full of joy and healthy. He wants us to live the more abundant life. God made us to want the same for our kids. God is willing and able to do a lot more for our kids than we are able.

In III John verse 2, the second part of the verse says, "even as thy soul prospereth." Both prosperity and health are contingent upon our soul prospering. That's the key to get your soul to prosper. This starts first in the mind, not in the physical realm.

Healthcare from God is free. God never brings sickness or disease. There are a few verses in the Word where it appears that that's the case, however, there are hundreds of verses where the will of God is healing and health. God's Word is perfect. God's original Word has no contradictions or errors in it.

Psalm 12:6

The words of the Lord *are* pure words: *as* silver
tried in a furnace of earth, purified seven times.

The word "pure" in the Hebrew is *tahor*. It means uncontaminated, unmixed, free from any evil contaminate. This verse says that God's Word is "purified seven times." The reason it says seven times is because Biblically the word "seven" represents spiritual perfection.

Metal that has not been fully purified leaves scum on molten metal which is called dross. God's Word has no dross or refuse in it. When it was originally written, from Genesis 1:1 to Revelation 22:21, God's Word had not one imperfection or lie in it. Man has added, deleted and/or changed God's Word in places. Therefore, you can thank man for any apparent errors or contradictions. In its original pureness and accuracy, it was nothing but the total truth in all its glory and power.

God wishes no one to be bed ridden, or ill, or live with a disease. God's health plan for His people is a healthy body and a sound mind. Health is to be enjoyed. Health, from God, is one of the great blessings of life from God. Our bodies are to perform without pain. God desires our parts and organs to function freely, undisturbed by germs and disease – a state in which all our bodily functions and parts consistently perform their job. All our organs and cells promote health. It's often hard to enjoy and have gladness for something you don't have, which is why we must recognize this promise from God and trust Him.

This promise I have claimed. It's a real joy and pleasure to sit and have no pain or any discomfort in my body. That is how God would have it. And I will carry on, enjoying a healthy body from God. It's often hard to enjoy and have gladness for something that we don't have, which is why we must recognize this promise from God and trust Him. This is our portion and it's from the hand of God.

The adversary, the devil, wants God's people to look defeated, miserable and down trodden in every area of their lives. If he can get God's people to look like failures, worried all the time and on the decline, then satan has succeeded. It's not good for you or for the outreach of God's Word. God never made a "burdened down" Christian. Then why be one? God is in there pitching for us to be healthy and enjoy life.

If you're healthy, continue to believe God and stay that way. If you're not, God wants you to change your thinking and get in alignment and harmony with what He says in His Word. God wants and wills for you to be healed completely.

Psalm 107:20

He sent His word, and healed them, and delivered *them* from their destructions.

God's will is that we are healed in every facet of our lives including the mental aspect. This is where we all need healing first, in our minds. Then, when we have a mind that believes, our healing takes place. Believing emanates from the mind. If we can get the mind sound, our physical body will follow suit. Health is mental, physical and spiritual. It's our own wrong thinking, our lack of care and unbelief, our own destructions, that we need to be delivered from. Worry ends where believing kicks in. We can have our health if we want it. We just have to give up the belief that we can't be healed and allow our desire to grow by the belief that we can and deserve to be healed because we are God's children. We as God's people must learn to overcome. We can have anything and do anything if we will just give up the thought that we can't. Believing is a matter that is between you and God alone. No one can believe for you. Just as you have to believe to receive eternal life, you must believe for health and prosperity. No one can do it for you.

Exodus 23: 25

And ye shall serve the Lord your God, and he
shall bless thy bread, and thy water; and I will
take sickness away from the midst of thee.

We receive deliverance by believing God, just as the people in the Word did. No one ever earns healing. You will never be good enough to earn something from God. If receiving something from God was dependent upon our goodness or our holiness, we would never receive anything from Him. We receive from God, by believing. God will take sickness away from you. When God takes sickness away, He does not give it back. When God takes away something and you trust Him you don't ever see it again. He removes it as far as the east is from the west.

God says He will personally bless your food and drink. It will be greater in quality and nutrition than any health food you could purchase. Remember it's also the water we drink. Who should have better food and water than God's kids? I'll take average food blessed by God any day, over good health food that is not sanctified.

This verse also says, "And ye shall serve the Lord your God." Sometimes when people hear that they should serve the Lord, they think of giving everything to the point of exhaustion. They think of running here and there to take care of people who have problems. They think of burning themselves out for the Lord.

That is not serving the Lord. Serving God is not a bondage or sacrifice. So, what is God's heart on serving Him?

Colossians 3:23 & 24

vs 23   And whatsoever ye do, do *it* heartily, as to the Lord, and not unto men;

vs 24   Knowing that of the Lord ye shall receive the reward of the inheritance: for ye serve the Lord Christ.

To serve God is to do everything that we do with our whole heart toward God. It is everything we do in the high ways and byways of life. It is enjoying all that God has given us. It is giving and receiving, loving and sharing and sowing and reaping. Of course, there are times of seriousness and solemnness. There are times for reflection and quietness. Serving God is an attitude of heart. To serve God is very healing mentally. We are to enjoy our food and drink, play, work, pray, be with our children, have our hobbies, play sports, take vacations, do all that we do with our WHOLE HEARTS toward God.

I Timothy 4:4 & 5

vs 4   For every creature of God *is* good, and nothing to be refused, if it be received with thanksgiving:

vs 5   For it is sanctified by the word of God
and prayer.

Food is to be received with thanksgiving. When you have a thankful heart to God, you have some food to eat. That doesn't mean it's mandatory to pray for every meal. Maybe sometimes we should quietly take a moment and receive it with thanksgiving. That's how I like to eat my food. Either way I receive it with thankfulness. Just don't have too much vain repetition of the same prayer, let it come from your heart. God has a lot of variety in life let's not be so religious with the same prayer. I may pray for the same thing often, but there is no script with it. God is our constant companion. He likes to hear from our hearts. By the way, God never thinks we're redundant when we say, "I love you," or "Thank you" to Him.

Exodus 15:26b

. . . for I *am* the Lord that healeth thee.

The four words "Lord that healeth thee" are two words in the Hebrew, *Jehovah-Rapha*. *Jehovah* means: God the immutable promise keeper and *Rapha* means: that heals. This is one of the names that God calls Himself. I like to look at it like a nickname God gave Himself, something He wants us to specifically see Him as.

All healing started with God. The very nature of God is to

heal. This very nature constitutes God. It's God's affection and His natural disposition to man. The records of healing in God's Word are there to help us believe for God's healing love. There is no reason to settle for less than God's best. If we have a sickness, why do we keep living with it when health is just a believing thought away? We need to grow and claim this promise of health. It seems too many of God's people are content to live with a sickness, and often more than one. And when we don't have the believing to receive our deliverance, let's be like the man who said, "Lord help thou my unbelief." He made up his mind healing was going to happen for his son. And I thank God that there are people today with the will and strength to do the same. We don't overcome our sicknesses, we overcome our unbelief.

Personally, I have no sickness, or any type of disease. I thank God for my health often. And, if I do catch something, I'm on it fast. Light slows down for me. I make sure I'm on talking terms with God. I nip it in the bud quick, because I know it is not the will of God to have, or to live with sickness of any kind. Do you ever want your child to be sick? God loves us a lot more than we will ever love our kids. God's limitless love has no bounds.

Jesus Christ was never sick a day in his life. He was tempted to be sick, but did not succumb to the temptation. In the record of Luke six, Jesus Christ heals the multitude.

Luke 6:17-19

vs 17   And he came down with them, and stood in the plain, and the company of his disciples, and a great multitude of people out of all Judea and Jerusalem, and from the sea coast of Tyre and Si-don, which came to hear him, and to be healed of their diseases;

vs 18   And they that were vexed with unclean spirits: and they were healed.

vs 19   And the whole multitude sought to touch him: for there went virtue out of him, and healed *them* all.

This virtue, this power is impossible to drain, or for it to ever run out. I don't know if the people got in line to touch him or exactly how it was done. However, people would have seen the physical healing taking place with their own eyes. They would have watched people, before and after them, be healed. It says in verse nineteen that the whole multitude sought to touch him. If we had been there to see this power, we would have wanted to touch him too! I would have wanted to touch Jesus Christ just for a double portion of good health. I'm not going to let Elisha have all the fun. What a wonderful and beautiful display of God's loving power this must have been. God has not changed.

Healing is just as available today as it was then. These people were not loved by God more than we are.

Isaiah 53:5

But *he was* wounded for our transgressions, *He*
was bruised for our iniquities: the chastisement
of our peace *was* upon him; and with his stripes
we are healed.

The verse says, "We ARE HEALED." Jesus Christ was the payment for our healing now, today, this moment. He went through horrendous torture and pain to accomplish our healing. He sacrificed his body so that we could have health. Do you think it was easy because he was the son of God? He was also a man. He experienced every ounce of pain and agony that they inflicted upon him. He knew that what he had to do would be horrific. And, because of that, only one time recorded in God's Word did Jesus Christ ever ask God if it was possible to do something another way.

Matthew 26:36 – 44

vs 36   Then cometh Jesus with them unto a
place called Gethsemane, and saith unto his disciples, "Sit ye here while I go and pray yonder".

vs 37   And He took with Him Peter and the two sons of Zebedee and began to be sorrowful and very heavy.

vs 38   Then saith He unto them, "My soul is exceeding sorrowful, even unto death: tarry ye here, and watch with me".

vs 39   And He went a little farther, and fell on His face, and prayed, saying, "Oh My Father, if it be possible, let this cup pass from me: nevertheless not as I will but as thou *wilt.*"

vs 40   And He cometh unto the disciples, and findeth them asleep, and saith unto Peter, "What, could ye not watch with me one hour?

vs 41   Watch and pray that ye enter not into temptation: the spirit indeed *is* willing, but the flesh *is* weak."

vs 42   He went away again the second time, and prayed saying, "O My Father, if this cup may not pass away from Me, except I drink it, Thy will be done."

vs 43   And He came and found them asleep
again: for their eyes were heavy.

vs 44   And He left them, and went away again,
and prayed the third time, saying the same
words.

The same account is also recorded in Mark 14:32 – 41 and
Luke 22:39 – 46.

Luke 22:42

Saying, Father, if thou be willing, remove this
cup from me: nevertheless not my will, but
thine, be done.

God showed Jesus Christ the torture and humiliation he
would have to endure. He asked God three times if there was any
other way to redeem mankind. Even during this short time, his
heart was to do God's will. Christ was just looking for another
way if at all possible. His heart was always, "Not my will, but
Thine be done." Jesus Christ always sets the standard for heart
and commitment.

Up to this point, Christ lived with great freedom in his life.
No one had ever laid a finger on Jesus Christ until he allowed it.
It was not until the last few days of his life that anyone ever in-
flicted any physical pain on him. And as a man, he felt pain as we

do. He had never been bound or incarcerated. He moved with freedom, everywhere God wanted him go.

Luke 22:44

And being in agony he prayed more earnestly:
and his sweat was as it were great drops of blood
falling down to the ground.

Jesus Christ knew he had to do the will of the Father in order to obtain our salvation. He loved God with all his heart and commitment. He also understood the love that God had for him.

Remember Christ's blood was spilt for our forgiveness so we could obtain eternal life. The physical beating and torture that he took was for our healing so that we could live life with a healthy body and mind. God did not HAVE to do this for us. He CHOSE to do this for us.

I Peter 2:24

Who [Jesus Christ] his own self bare our sins in
his own body on the tree, that we, being dead to
sins, should live unto righteousness: by whose
stripes ye were healed.

It meant a great deal to God to have His son go through all the pain and suffering so that we could enjoy health. It was a monumental sacrifice to Him. And now, because of what God through Christ did, we have eternal life and can claim forgiveness and physical healing. God did all this to deliver you and me in every way. It is God's great love for us. So then, since God loved us so much to do all this for us, we should love ourselves and likewise never criticize or condemn ourselves.

Luke 22:45

And when he rose up from prayer, and was
come to his disciples, he found them sleeping
for sorrow.

Jesus Christ found them sleeping for sorrow. Christ told them what was going to happen to him which produced great disappointment and pain of mind for these men. They did not want to hear Christ tell them that he was going to be arrested and crucified. How hurt, how deeply grieved and full of sorrow these men must have been knowing that were going to lose the physical presence of Jesus Christ. The hurt and emotions must have been so deep to the heart and soul of these men. They were going to lose the one person who loved them more than anyone ever had before. At times, when the pressure is really on and it's a situation you can do nothing about, I think it's natural for all of us to just want to sleep.

The following verses are a few of my favorites.

John 15:9

As the Father hath loved me, so have I loved
you: continue ye in my love.

John 16:27

For the Father himself loveth you, because ye
have loved me, and have believed that I came
out from God.

God is wearing His heart on His sleeve when he says, "For
the Father Himself loves you." The word "loveth" in the Greek
is *phileo*; it's human love. It is never used of man's love to God. It
means to be fond of, have affection for, to be the closest of friends.
The more you work God's Word, the greater His love appears.

John 17:23

I in them, and thou in me, that they may be
made perfect in one; and that the world may
know that thou has sent me, and hast loved
them, as thou hast loved me.

This verse says that God loves you as He loved Christ. That
is more than the heart can process.

Jesus Christ had the love of God in his heart. His life was one
of healing God's people. You will never see a verse in God's Word

where Jesus said, "Oh, good, she is sick and God is testing her."

In the following record Christ is going with Jairus to heal his daughter. As he moved among the people many were gathering around him and touching him.

Mark 5:24 – 34

vs 24   And *Jesus* went with him [Jairus]; and much people followed him, and thronged him.

vs 25   And a certain women, which had an issue of blood twelve years

vs 26   And had suffered many things of many physicians, [still true today] and had spent all that she had, and was nothing better, but rather grow worse,

For twelve years she lived with this issue. She had years of reinforced wrong thinking to overcome. She spent all she had, she lost it all. She was totally broke and getting sicker.

vs 27   When she heard of Jesus, came in the press behind, and touched his garment.

vs 28   For she said, if I may touch but his clothes, I shall be whole.

The woman got this in her thinking from somewhere. Why was it at this point she was able to give up the belief of not being healed? Do you remember the multitude that sought to touch him? She had heard of people being healed by touching Jesus Christ. She gave up the belief "I can't, " to "If I may touch his clothes, I shall be whole." She had heard enough to believe. The Word of God builds believing for deliverance. And we have to hear enough of God's Word to build our believing to the point of deliverance. Her worry and fear ended when her believing kicked in. Believing is sparked and ignited by love. And her hope of deliverance fueled them both. Wherever Christ is, there is love and deliverance.

> vs 29   And straightway the fountain of her
> blood was dried up; and she felt in *her* body that
> she was healed of that plague.

> vs 30   And Jesus immediately knowing in him-
> self that virtue [Greek: *dunamis* = power] had
> gone out of him, turned him about in the press,
> and said, Who touched my clothes.

God let him know by revelation that healing had gone out of his clothing.

> vs 31   And his disciples said unto him, Thou
> seest the multitude thronging thee, and sayest
> thou, Who touched me?

> vs 32   And he looked round about to see her
> who had done this thing.

> vs 33   But the woman fearing and trembling,
> knowing what was done in her, came and fell
> down before him, and told him all the truth.

I would have loved to hear her story of deliverance which she shared with Christ.

She spent all she had – she lost it all. When we get sick or hurt the first place we should go is God. She spent all her energy and effort going to the world first. When I get sick or hurt the first place I go is to God. And if my believing is not there, I do what I need to do to bring believing deliverance to myself while continuing to pray and thank God for His help.

> vs 34   And he said unto her, Daughter, thy faith
> hath made thee whole; go in peace, and be
> whole of thy plague.

She not only received her health, but she was made whole. To be made whole means mentally, emotionally and spiritually.

Just as III John 2 says, God's wish or will is for us to have prosperity and health in every category. God's will is God's Word is God's way.

Isaiah 55:11

So shall my word be that goeth forth out of my mouth: it shall not return unto me void, but it shall accomplish that which I please, and it shall prosper *in the thing* whereto I sent it.

God's Word never returns void. The word "void" means: to no purpose, without effect. God's Word will accomplish that which pleases God. It will do the same for us as it did for the people in the Word who believed.

This word "prosper" means to go through, to push forward, to reach the goal, to accomplish successfully. God's Word gets sent out by us speaking it and living it. And, if we can write about it well and show some of God's heart and will for His people, that's part of God's Word being sent. God has no feet but our feet to bring His Word to the rest of the world. God's will is always health and prosperity for His people.

SPIRITUAL GOODIES
For God Sent His Word and Healed Them

- Reading God's Word heals your heart unlike anything else.

- If we could see inside some Christians' minds and see their spiritual thinking, do you think it would be like passing through a sleeping person's mind?

- The best key in bringing relief from selfishness is giving.

- God's peace is the only thing that will free you from internal commotion and unrest.

- Having sin consciousness and thinking that you will never be good enough has stopped more of us from walking with God than perhaps anything else.

- God's heart truly is an open book. If you want to know God's heart, you have to know His Word.

- It's the Word of God that nourishes and replenishes the soul.

- I used to think love wasn't everything. My God, life is empty and worthless without it.

- Half the people say love does not last in marriage. It's like brushing your teeth; it's something you have to live and do daily.

- What would you depend on or rely upon more than who you would pray to?

- We are part of God's family and the only thing that is going to hold us together is God's Word and God's love.

- You won't help anyone more than when you help them with the Word of God.

- Of all the wonderful principles in God's Word, believing prayer may open the door further than any other thing in understanding the Word and heart of God.

- In light of spiritual food, the best brand is nothing but the truth.

- Frequently, thank God for an open door of utterance. And thank Him for more boldness.

- Inevitably we will talk about what we love, but some people love to talk about what they hate.

- When it seems there is no way, the love of God will find a way.

Chapter Four

Forgiveness and the Malefactors

Jesus Christ is the only man to ever walk the face of the earth that never needed forgiveness from anyone. He never had an evil thought nor did he ever have to forgive himself. He never had a fear, or ever feared anything his whole life. All he ever did was love and forgive. Christ showed kindness to many, many people. And to me, his greatest act of loving forgiveness was choosing to hang on the cross.

He could have had 72,000 angels come and help him. But instead of claiming that help, he said, "But how then shall the scriptures be fulfilled." That is THE example of loving God. Do you know anybody on talking terms with God like that?

When Jesus Christ was hanging on the cross, the physical pain and suffering he went through would have been absolutely excruciating. Human hands have more nerve endings in them than any other part of our bodies. The hand has approximately one thousand nerve endings per square inch and the sole of the foot has approximately one thousand three hundred per square inch. He endured more than any man ever has, or will. Our Savior had nails the size of spikes driven through his hands and his feet. The best of us could not have endured the half of what he did and yet he forgave as he hung there on that tree.

Luke 23:32 – 47

vs 32   And there were also two other, malefactors, led with him to be put to death.

vs 33   And when they were come to the place, which is called Calvary, there they crucified him, and the malefactors, one on the right hand, and the other on the left.

vs 34   Then said Jesus, Father, forgive them; for they know not what they do. And they parted his raiment, and cast lots.

Jesus Christ, hanging on that cross said, "Forgive them." He forgave the very people who had nailed him to that tree. They were the ones killing him. Jesus Christ always set the standard and the precedent on forgiveness, not you or me. Jesus Christ made the standard as a rule or basis of comparison in measuring all pardoning. Christ is *the* model to follow when it comes to forgiveness. We are to pattern our lives after his. Any other standard could lead you asunder.

Don't we want to be more like Christ? He was God's favorite kid you know. The thought never crossed his mind to not forgive. And if there ever was a time he could have been unforgiving, this was it. Christ pardoned to the degree that he loved. His choice was always the same decision – to forgive.

> vs 35   And the people stood beholding. And the rulers also with them derided him, saying, He saved others; let him save himself, if he be Christ, the chosen of God.

The world will never understand Jesus Christ. They will mock him until he comes back. And he is coming Back! Jesus Christ is coming back as KING OF KINGS AND LORD OF LORDS. They won't spit on him, beat him, or mock him then.

> vs 36   And the soldiers also mocked him, coming to him, and offering him vinegar,

> vs 37   And saying, If thou be the king of the Jews, save thyself.

At that moment, Jesus Christ is offering these men eternal life. He's dying on that cross for the salvation and forgiveness of all mankind. You may have some horrific things to forgive, but nothing like Jesus Christ was willing to forgive these people for at that place and time.

> vs 38   And a superscription also was written
> over him in letters of Greek, and Latin, and
> Hebrew, THIS IS THE KING OF THE JEWS.

This was written in all three major languages of the day and time. Anyone present would have been able to read the mocking accusation.

> vs 39   And one of the malefactors which were
> hanged railed on him, saying, If thou be Christ,
> save thyself and us.

A malefactor is an evil worker. He is one that breaks the laws of God, and the laws of the land. This man did not want Christ's forgiveness.

> vs 40   But the other answering rebuked him,
> saying, Dost not thou fear God, seeing thou art
> in the same condemnation?

> vs 41   And we indeed justly; for we receive the
> due reward of our deeds: but this man hath
> done nothing amiss.

> vs 42   And he said unto Jesus, Lord, remember
> me when thou comest into thy kingdom.

The second malefactor wanted forgiveness and he knew he needed it. And after all, is not this the very reason Christ was hanging on that tree, so that we could receive forgiveness and appropriate eternal life? This man only had a few hours of life left and he changed his eternity forever. The greatest thing God did was offer us eternal life. It's God's greatest act of loving forgiveness. The greatest thing we could ever do for someone is offer them eternal life.

This malefactor called Jesus Christ Lord. He gave Christ great respect in saying that. He believed Christ was the way to eternal life, even though the man was guilty of breaking the law. Sometimes when people are dying, their heart softens. Eternal life can come at the most likely and unlikely places and time.

> vs 43   And Jesus said unto him, Verily I say unto
> thee, To day shalt thou be with me in paradise.

In Christ's dying moments, he gave eternal life to one more person. What do you think it meant to this man at this hour in his life? Imagine what it was like for that man to know that he was forgiven and that he was going to live forever. I feel safe to say this was the most thankful this man had ever been. He was the last person recorded that Christ forgave.

> vs 44   And it was about the sixth hour, and
> there was a darkness over all the earth until the
> ninth hour.

The sixth hour was noon their time. From noon to three in the afternoon there was darkness over all the earth. This darkness was the absence of light. It was the absence of physical light and the absence of the light of the world, Jesus Christ. Even being a believer it might cause you to have awe and tremble.

> vs 45   And the sun was darkened, and the veil of the temple was rent in the midst.

> vs 46   And when Jesus had cried with a loud voice, he said, Father, into thy hands I commend my spirit: and having said thus, he gave up the ghost.

Verse forty-six says Christ GAVE UP the ghost. Those who crucified him did not take his life. He, Christ gave up his life. What kept him hanging on that tree? It was his love for God and his love for you and me. Giving one's life is the greatest act of love one man could do for another.

John 15:13

Greater love hath no man than this, that a man lay down his life for his friends.

You can have no greater love. It's what Christ did for us. God's Word always sets the standard and precedent for love and forgiveness.

Ecclesiastes 12:7

Then shall the dust return to the earth as it was:
and the spirit shall return unto God who gave it.

If the Lord tarries and you die, your spirit will also go back to God who gave it. God raised Christ from the dead three days later. So his body did not return to dust or see corruption.

Luke 23:47

vs 47   Now when the centurion saw what was
done, he glorified God, saying, Certainly this
was a righteous man.

Whenever you are speaking and living God's Word, you never know who is watching and listening. God will work within you in the most likely and unlikely places and times.

2 Timothy 4:2

Preach the word; be instant in season, out of
season; reprove, rebuke, exhort with all longsuf-
fering and doctrine.

The words "in season" mean: when the opportunity arises, at the opportune time, seasonably. You just know it on the inside, and you speak it on the outside.

The words "out of season" mean: It's not conducive to speak, unseasonable. Spiritually, if the weather is good or bad, we speak the Word. What are others saying that is more important than God and His Word? Come on, most of the conversations that happen today are usually just a bunch of carnal, earthly, waste land and vain words. No one is being built up by what the world says. When we leave a conversation, we should be a lot more concerned about what God thinks, than what anybody else thought.

There are times I wish I had spoken the Word, and that opportunity is gone forever. The people in those situations may have appeared like they liked me more, but I like living and moving and having my being in God. And when we live that way, we feel a lot better about ourselves before God, knowing we did what we believed He wanted. That way I don't have to have those thoughts and feelings that I need to forgive myself. Sometimes we might think that people will like us more if we do not speak God's Word. If that's our state of affairs, we need to wake up. If you like being a witness, you know what I'm talking about. Make sure you don't judge yourself, and don't be too hard on yourself, we all need to grow. Condemnation is never a happy road to travel either. Sometimes we just do the best we can and let God do the rest. But, don't let fear stop you from helping people or speaking His Word. Remember someone told you about God and His Word.

Luke 6:36

Be ye therefore merciful, as your Father also is
merciful.

Mercy is very relieving. Mercy is God's withheld judgment,
punishment or wrath. When you were growing up and you really blew it and should have been spanked, but you were not,
that was mercy. I thank God I had plenty of mercy growing up.
Now, as children mimic their parents, we are to follow our Father's lead. We are to be the children of our Father and manifest
mercy to others. Don't allow your heart to become desensitized
to mercy and forgiveness.

Luke 6:37

Judge not, and ye shall not be judged: condemn
not, and ye shall not be condemned: forgive,
and ye shall be forgiven:

We are not the presiding judge, neither judging for or against.
We are not the one who determines a person's heart color, black,
white or somewhere in between. The word "condemn" means to
pronounce judgment against or to condemn. We should condemn no one. This word "forgive" means that you remit the punishment, and you do it with some graciousness in your soul. It
can include some covering at times. The love of God covers.

I John 3:20

For if our heart condemn us, God is greater than
our heart, and knoweth all things.

This word "condemn" is in the sense that we blame and find
fault with ourselves. We accuse and think ill of ourselves to the
end that we have no confidence in God or ourselves. Condemnation robs more of our believing than we know. It is knowing
and believing what Christ did for us and who we are in Christ
that gives us confidence.

This verse says, "If your heart condemns you." And, your heart
certainly will, that's why God has it in here. Thank God for the rest
of the verse. God knows why we are doing it, and He will help us
over come. God is greater than our heart. Isn't that comforting?

I John 3:21

Beloved, if our heart condemn us not, then have
we confidence toward God.

When we condemn ourselves, we look at ourselves as being
worthless and not good enough. We think, "What could I do?"
When we have these thoughts of condemnation, we don't have
confidence. A condemning heart has no confidence in God.
Thank God He is greater than our heart and can help us overcome. When we know and believe we are forgiven, then we have

confidence toward God. And confidence issues in trust which brings you to believe.

John 3:17

For God sent not his Son into the world to condemn the world; but that the world through him
might be saved.

God is not condemning any of His kids. Remember He is going to have us come live with Him forever. God wants us all to know we are a part of His family. God gave us emotions. If we have positive good thinking according to God's Word, good feelings will follow.

I John 1:9

If we confess our sins, [broken fellowship] he is
faithful and just to forgive us our sins, [broken fel-
lowship] and to cleanse us from all unrighteousness.

Just genuinely be sorry and thank God for forgiveness when you blow it, and move on. That's what Jesus Christ did for us. Even though we sin and fall short of what God's Word says, we don't have to have condemnation, guilt and self-reproach. We all have our faults and short comings and will until Christ returns. However we DO NOT have to live with accusation and sentence of self. Don't let that part of what Christ did for you be in vain. Christ paid for all of our mental prisons as well. Heaven is a place where no one will ever need forgiveness again, but in the meantime, claim your forgiveness because of what Jesus Christ did for you and refuse to walk in guilt and condemnation.

Jesus Christ's life story is one of forgiveness. He came making it available to whoever wants it. To receive eternal life, you have to be forgiven. We all have a choice – do we want forgiveness or not. Jesus Christ was not here condemning the world. He came to save the world. Jesus Christ's life was about eternal forgiveness. He came to make it available to live with God forever in a place where there is no death or fear of anything ever again.

Revelation 21:4

And God shall wipe away all tears from their
eyes; and there shall be no more death, neither
sorrow, nor crying, neither shall there be any
more pain: for the former things are passed away.

God has given us the greatest thing we could ever have to look forward to. And he gave us this eternal life by the sacrifice of Jesus Christ.

Acts 5:31

Him [Jesus Christ] hath God exalted with his
right hand to be a Prince and a Saviour, for to
give repentance to Israel, and forgiveness of sins.

Acts 13:38

Be it known unto you therefore, men and brethren, that through this man is preached unto you
the forgiveness of sins:

Jesus Christ came to give forgiveness of sins. Let us live in
the freedom that gives. It's personally yours and mine to have.
Forgiveness is a place that you are wanted. It is a place where you
know you are among the body of Christ where you belong. Forgiveness is where you feel at home. It is where you are accepted
– a place we all need. Furthermore, it is our privilege to preach it
today. And it is no less important to live in the freedom it brings.

Forgiveness is a want and need we have in our souls. When
we believe we are forgiven it fulfills that need. Forgiveness is a
place where you have acceptance and long for.

Acts 13:39

And by him all that believe are justified from all
things, from which ye could not be justified by
the law of Moses.

When you believe, you are justified. Justified means, "Just as
if you had never sinned." The freedom that the forgiveness of God
gives is one of the greatest keys there is to living the more abundant life. We are not destitute of any of God's loving forgiveness.

SPIRITUAL GOODIES
For Forgiveness and the Malefactors

- God's unconditional love is the freest thing in life there is.

- How loved we are by God has nothing to do with our performance or conduct. No one ever earns God's love. Before God ever made man, He decided to love us. We are loved by God in spite of our frailties and our inadequacies.

- Your forgiveness toward someone can be more of a healing balm than you know.

- Two things I enjoyed in my youth: when school was dismissed and the judge said, "Dismissed."

- When you forgive, more good comes to you over the course of your life than you will ever know.

- Here are a few things that mean absolutely nothing to God: your race, pedigree, nationality, the color of your skin and your denomination. God wants to know what's inside the heart.

- Wounds to your heart which are caused by another or perhaps by yourself, take time to heal.

- Christ forgave freely, with no expectation or regard for himself.

- When Christ returns no one is going to spit on him, ridicule him or beat a crown of thornes on his head. He is coming back as King of Kings and Lord of Lords.

- Jesus Christ's life was one of endless forgiveness. It's still taking place today.

- No one has or ever will earn or merit God's forgiveness.

- The love of God is the most powerful incentive there is. It's what sent Christ to the cross.

- Jesus Christ never had any repercussions associated with not forgiving.

- The Word of God sets the standard on what forgiveness is. How would you even know how to forgive without knowing what God's Word says? How could you love God without knowing His Word?

- God asks us to forgive. The respect you have for Him will determine the outcome.

- God is faithful and just to forgive us our sin.

- Any fool can withhold his forgiveness.

- If you love God, when it's in the power of your hand to forgive, you will.

- There is not one of us that does not receive more from God than we deserve – the godless or the godly.

- Of all the things God has done for us, what could be more valued than eternal life.

- God's love blocks the preceptors of fear.

- If you don't think God is blessing you as He should, maybe He should bless you in light of what you deserve.

- In God's eyes the blind are those who can't spiritually see.

- The most epic day in history was when Christ rose from the dead. The next is when he comes back.

- What a wonderful thought to have that you will never have to forgive God.

- God has shown us vast kindness. We only know the beginning of it. When Christ returns we will understand the other 99%.

Chapter Five

Health is God's Will For Your Life

It's NEVER, EVER God's will that we are sick. There is no place in God's Word that says He wants us to be sick or unhealthy! God loves us and always wants and wishes for us to be healthy and prosperous. God only wants the best for His people. Just reading God's Word is healing to our bodies and souls. And, filling our minds with verses on healing will build our trust and believing toward God. God's Word will build our desire and help us overcome the weakness in our thinking that we will never get healed. We need to change our minds to believe what God's Word says about health and healing.

Romans 12:2

And be not conformed to this world: but be ye
transformed by the renewing of your mind, that
ye may prove what is that good, and acceptable,
and perfect, will of God.

We do not want to be conformed to this world. The world tells you all the things that you cannot have, be or do. God's Word promises us life more than abundant in every category. Renewing your mind transforms you into someone who proves the good, acceptable and perfect will of God. The word "transformed" is the Greek word *metamorphoo* from which we get the word metamorphosis. In essence, we can morph from a caterpillar into a beautiful butterfly that is not bound to the earth. Our believing can take flight. We can change from someone who did not care about God to someone who loves God and His people.

Renewing our minds with God's Word is invaluable to our health. It's only God and His Word that will help a person overcome the funk of wrong thinking and bad mental habits. We develop well-worn paths in our minds that only the power of the Word can break through. These worn paths are the bad habits of unbelief. We are either believing positively or we are believing that which is negative. We either get positive results or negative results. We need to wake up to the truth that God's desire is for us to be healed. And, one of the greatest ways I know to replace these negative ruts in our minds is to write down verses on healing and carry them with us. Then take the time to look at the verses often throughout our day. Nothing will make us stronger or build our believing like God's Word itself. Remember the centurion heard about Christ first, then he believed.

Proverbs 3:5 – 8

vs 5   Trust in the LORD with all thine heart; and lean not unto thine own understanding.

vs 6   In all thy ways acknowledge him, and he shall direct thy paths.

vs 7   Be not wise in thine own eyes: fear [respect, reverence] the LORD, and depart from evil.

vs 8   It shall be health to thy navel, and marrow to thy bones.

In verse eight using the word "navel" is a figure of speech called *synecdoche*. *Synecdoche* is using a part of something to stand for the whole. The navel stands for the whole body. Whenever God uses a figure of speech, it's always for emphasis. He is calling our attention to something important – listen up! God's Word is emphasizing that His Word is healing to the **whole** body. The marrow is where the blood is manufactured. That's about as important as it gets! The bones must be kept healthy in order for the physical body to be whole.

Proverbs 4:20 – 22

vs 20   My son, attend to my words; incline thine ear unto my sayings.

vs 21   Let them not depart from thine eyes;
keep them in the midst of thine heart.

vs 22   For they are life unto those that find
them, and health to all their flesh.

God's words give life. The word "life" is the Hebrew word *chay* which means: alive, fresh, strong, life giving, reviving. God's Word has life in it. It is a living word. God's Word literally gives healing to the physical body. It restores and cures the body. There is more power in God's Word than we know.

I have needed little physical healing in my life. I have physical health and am thankful to God for it. My need early in life was to have soundness of mind. The bars that imprison the mind can be the most tormenting. I was born again at four or five years old. I always knew I had eternal life, and regardless of how I lived I was heaven bound and all hell could not stop me from going. I knew I was a son of God and my sins would all be forgiven. I knew full well what Christ had accomplished for me. Some of the people I read about in the Word often remind me of how I used to live. God refers to it as the old man, our carnal and sensual way of living. Like the son who left his father and brother. Or like the malefactor hanging on the cross next to Christ who said, "we receive the due reward of our deeds . . . remember me when thou comest into thy kingdom." It's God's Word that changes our thinking, to bring healing to our lives. I'm very thankful I am not where I used to be, but we all need to continue to grow. However I sure like anticipating and looking forward to the future. The future is as bright as the promises of God. No man could come close to promising you what God does.

If God never sent His Word, we would all be lost forever. The reason we can believe God is because of His Word. It's the only way we can know God. We can get no closer to God's heart than His Word. It's how He lets us know who He is. It is how we understand Him, how He reveals Himself to us.

It's our own fears that bind the hands of God. Fear defeats the promises of God. Fear always enslaves. It always imprisons the individual seeking deliverance. It ties the hands of God in our lives. In our dreams and longings, fear stops us from doing what we want to do. Action cures fear. Non-action strengthens fear.

God calls us believers because that is what He expects of us. A lot of what we need is deliverance from our own negative unbelieving attitude. Have you ever really noticed the verse in the word that says believing is a law?

Romans 3:27

Where is boasting then? It is excluded. By what law? of works? Nay: but by the law of faith [believing].

The verse says, "by the law of faith." The word "faith" is the Greek word *pistis*, which is believing. This verse documents that believing is a law. What we believe is the governing factor in our lives. It's the determining law in every area of our life. It's why we accomplish or don't accomplish anything in our lives. We are all where we are today because of our believing. And, do you know what? Tomorrow you will go wherever your believing thoughts take you, because it is a law. You can look around and see why people are where they're at. They are where their positive or negative believing has taken them. Verse twenty-eight states that we are justified by our faith or believing.

Romans 3:28

Therefore we conclude that a man is justified by faith without the deeds of the law.

When you believed in Jesus Christ you became eternally justified – it's a one time occurrence. You stand before God justified, or just as if you never sinned. Then you have the freedom to live like hell or live like heaven. You can believe God's Word or you can be negative and reap the consequences of your unbelief. You can have prosperity and health from God; you just have to give up the belief that you can't. It's only God's Word that will build the desire and will to overcome.

When we doubt that we can believe like the people in the Word did, we need to overcome those thoughts. We can have and do anything we want. The world is so conducive and has so conditioned us not to believe God. This causes us to be weak in believing. We think that God's promises are for people like Moses, Abraham, Paul and John. However, God's Word is just as available to us as it was to them. God is no respecter of persons. He loves us no less or more than He loved those men. God respects and honors believing. God wants us to believe for health and prosperity because He loves us.

3 John 1:2

Beloved, I wish above all things that thou mayest prosper and be in health, even as thy soul prospereth.

We must note very carefully that both prosperity and health are dependent upon the phrase, "even as thy soul prospereth." These promises are contingent upon, "even as your soul prospers." That is the hinge prosperity and health ride on. The Word of God is the only thing that causes the soul to prosper. So the key to prospering the soul, which is our mind, will, thinking, our smarts, is the Word of God living in our lives by way of the renewed mind. It's light that dispels darkness. It's a sound mind and believing heart that receives prosperity and health from God. The only thing that changes the old man is the Word of God. We have to put on the new man to change the old man. Our old habits and old thinking did and do not do the Word or believe the Word.

God's Word in our heart and mind builds believing. It's fear and the belief that we can't that defeats us. It's by believing we overcome. There is no other way. How we look at the situation with which we are confronted with right now, will determine the outcome.

1 John 5:4

For whatsoever is born of God overcometh the
world: and this is the victory that overcometh
the world, even our faith [believing].

We obtain eternal life by believing. We overcome poverty and sickness by our believing. We need to hear enough of God's Word to build and give our hearts the strength it needs to overcome. When it comes to health, this is the best attitude I know.

Philippians 4:13

I can do all things through Christ which
strengtheneth me.

"Can't" is a bad four letter word. (Sometimes I still think the word "work" is bad word too. But I digress from my point, lol.) The "I can do" attitude causes you to prevail with God's strength. If you want health, you fill your mind with all the wonderful verses and records on health, healing, wholeness and soundness of body and mind you can find. Fill your mind with God's healing love. Think of all the common everyday people in the Word just like us who got healed, and stayed delivered. Just like some-where along the line you heard enough to believe to become born again, they heard enough of God's Word to believe for their healing. Most of us don't even know when we got born again.

Here is another beautiful record of healing in God's Word.

Acts 3:1 – 12

vs 1   Now Peter and John went up together into the temple at the hour of prayer, being the ninth hour [about 3 p.m.].

vs 2   And a certain man lame from his moth-er's womb was carried, whom they laid daily at the gate of the temple which is called Beautiful, to ask alms of them that entered into the temple;

vs 3   Who seeing Peter and John about to go into the temple asked an alms.

vs 4   And Peter, fastening his eyes upon him with John, said, Look on us.

vs 5   And he gave heed unto them, expecting to receive something of them.

The man EXPECTED to receive something from them. He was believing.

vs 6   Then Peter said, Silver and gold have I
none; but such as I have give I thee: In the name
of Jesus Christ of Nazareth rise up and walk.

vs 7   And he took him by the right hand, [the
right hand is the hand of blessing in the bible]
and lifted him up: and immediately his feet and
ankle bones received strength.

vs 8   And he leaping up stood, and walked,
and entered with them into the temple, walking,
and leaping, and praising God.

If it were you or I, we would have been walking and leaping and praising God too. Some of us might have looked like
we needed some mental healing too. Man, cart wheels and flips,
summer salts, shoot, I would have become an acrobat.

vs 9   And all the people saw him walking and
praising God:

There is no better witness than your own testimony – a walking and leaping miracle.

Vs 10   And they knew that it was he which sat
for alms at the Beautiful gate of the temple:
and they were filled with wonder and amazement at that which had happened unto him.

How could anyone not be filled with wonder and amazement. The people saw him often at the gate. Man, to see somebody as messed up as this, and then see them leaping around praising God, that would be exciting. This was a man who was lame from his mother's womb. He was born lame. Many people would have seen this man and known him his whole life. He would not have to tell people, "Look what God did for me!" Although, I'm sure he did.

> vs 11   And as the lame man which was healed
> held Peter and John, all the people ran
> together unto them in the porch that is called
> Solomon's, greatly wondering.

He held Peter and John; he was so blessed and happy he didn't want to let them go. If it were us I don't think we would have wanted to let go either. Think how thankful you would be.

> vs 12   And when Peter saw it, he answered
> unto the people, Ye men of Israel, why marvel
> ye at this? or why look ye so earnestly on us, as
> though by our own power or holiness we had
> made this man to walk?

Peter is giving God the glory as he rightly should. After all that's where the power came from. This man had been waiting for over forty years, his whole life, for this miracle of healing.

Acts 4:22

For the man was above forty years old, on
whom this miracle of healing was shewed.

I can't speak for anyone else, but I would think that one of
the hardest things to overcome would be an infirmity you were
born with, rather than one you got later on in life. However, believing is still the key to receiving regardless. Honestly, what do
I know concerning that matter? That man's heart longings and
dreams came true that day. God's unconditional love of healing came to this man that day. God was pleased with the man at
the Gate Beautiful that day because he pleased God by believing
Him. Believing is a thing that we should desire to grow up in.
The greatest men and women who have ever lived are the ones
who have believed God.

Hebrews 11:6

But without faith *it is* impossible to please *him*:
for he that cometh to God must believe that he
is, and *that* he is a rewarder of them that diligently seek him.

A person's unbelief does not please God. Deliverance from
unbelief is available. We do not have to live in unbelief if we
don't want to. We can choose to believe God. John Wesley said,
"God does nothing except in response to believing prayer."

Proverbs 23:7a

For as he thinketh in his heart, so is he . . .

On that day this man changed the image he had carried of himself for over forty years. This verse, the lame man lived that day. He gave up the belief, "I can't." Believing is your receipt and assurance of no failure for you. He changed that day what he had been looking at for decades. What is it that made this man change his expectation of life that day? He believed God in this area for the first time in his life.

Matthew 9:29b

According to your faith be it unto you.

The man at the gate was laid there daily because of his believing. He was where he was the day of his deliverance because of his believing. And he continued in his future wherever his believing took him. He believed that God would heal him in the name of Jesus Christ.

Acts 4:12

Neither is there salvation in any other: for there
is none other name [Jesus Christ] under heaven
given among men, whereby we must be saved.

Using the two words, "neither and none," is a double negative for emphasis. It's in his name and his name alone that we receive salvation. God tells and sets the standard for eternal life. No one else does. We cannot attribute evil to God by thinking or saying, "Why does God save some and not others?" God gave everyone freedom of will. Man decides if he wants to go to heaven, not God.

There are hundreds of places in God's Word where we can see and read that God wants His people healthy and healed. Health is always God's will for His people. However, sometimes God's people do not rise to the believing promises of His Word and other times it takes them a little longer to get to the point of believing for deliverance. Therefore, we must always remember that we are never to be critical of those who are sick or need physical healing. Christ was always building people up, and helping them get to point they could believe when needed. Christ always required believing on the part of the individual seeking deliverance. Somebody had to believe. Let's be the people who say, "I CAN." I CAN BELIEVE! I WILL BELIEVE! I DO BELIEVE!

SPIRITUAL GOODIES
For Health is God's Will for Your Life

- The statement is often made, "If God loves us why is there so much suffering in the world?" The answer is because of People's unbelief. The devil, NOT God, brings death, sickness and poverty. All the floods, hurricanes and storms come from the devil. God gets blamed for most of the stuff the devil does. All evil ultimately comes from the devil. No one will ever be God's judge.

- It's important to God where you are, but He is more concerned with where you are going.

Chapter Six

Forgiveness and Health

There is a beautiful connection between forgiveness of sins and health in God's Word. It makes perfect sense, because living in unforgiveness is bitterness to the soul. It is sickness to the heart and soul of a man or a woman, like disease is to the body. God's will in His perfect love for us is that we are forgiven and live in health. He wants us spiritually clean and mentally and physically well in our lives.

So before we take a look at forgiveness and health together, let's look at the incredible forgiveness that God has in His heart for us. It stands alone in its beauty and accuracy depicting God's love for His people.

God is the Great Forgiver. He sacrificed His only begotten son, who never sinned, so that we could be forgiven. And by that, He made us forgivable. God gives forgiveness from His heart to us. He forgives all our offences and remits all our sins. God calls us blameless. God has completely released us and freed us of having to be sin conscious if we want to live it. If we preach sin all the time, that's what people are going to do. It is not our fault we were born into sin. We came from "the factory" with that sin nature. God does not impute sin to you, or treat you, or deal with you as a sinner. We are sons of God our Father. We are forgiven, we are no longer held accountable. We have no trespasses or debt that our Father has not already forgiven us for.

It's a wonderful blessing to see all the unique ways and forms God chooses to use the word "forgive" in His Word. They are: forgive, forgiveness, forgiven, forgiving, forgiveth, forgiveness's, forgave, forgavest, forgivable and forgiver. (A woman once told me that "forgiver" was pronounced "forgive her.")

Let's take a look at some of these words in God's Word.

I John 1:9

If we confess our sins, he is faithful and just to forgive us our sins, and to cleanse us from all unrighteousness.

Ephesians 1:7

In whom we have redemption through his blood, the forgiveness of sins, according to the riches of his grace;

Colossians 2:13

And you, being dead in your sins and the un-circumcision of your flesh, hath he quickened together with him, having <u>forgiven</u> you all trespasses;

Ephesians 4:32

And be ye kind one to another, tenderhearted, <u>forgiving</u> one another, even as God for Christ's sake hath forgiven you.

Psalm 103:3

Who <u>forgiveth</u> all thine iniquities; who healeth all thy diseases;

Daniel 9:9

To the Lord our God belong mercies and <u>forgivenesses</u>, though we have rebelled against him;

Luke 7:42

And when they had nothing to pay, he frankly <u>forgave</u> them both. Tell me therefore, which of them will love him most?

Psalm 78:38

But he, being full of compassion, <u>forgave</u> their iniquity, and destroyed them not: yea, many a time turned he his anger away, and did not stir up all his wrath.

Psalm 99:8a

Thou answeredst them, O LORD our God: thou wast a God that <u>forgavest</u> them.

God's disposition is to forgive and forget. Who else has the willingness or who else is so willful to forgive like God? Or who is so inclined like Him? It is wrong for us to carry thoughts of guilt and unworthiness in our hearts and souls, because we have been released from all thoughts of shame and regret. We are no longer bound to these thoughts. God Himself has excused us from every weakness and every fault. We have been released from the penalty of sin. Christ paid our debt in full. We have been absolved from having to suffer any punishment. He left nothing undone. Christ bore our sins because we could not. The pardoning of our sin is a great thing to be thankful for. After all, how else could we obtain eternal life without being forgiven?

Philippians 3:13

Brethren, I count not myself to have appre-
hended: but this one thing I do, forgetting those
things which are behind, and reaching forth
unto those things which are before,

Do you know what brings stress and pain to our lives? Reliving our sins in our minds does. Rehearsing and refreshing the
sins of the past causes us anguish. What sins of our past would
be of any value or worth remembering? The brightest future you
could have is to forget the past and move ahead believing the
promises of God. Any other kind of future would be worthless
and unfulfilling.

Isaiah 43:25

I, even I, am he that blotteth out thy transgressions for mine own sake, and will not remember
thy sins.

God forgets our sin which man somehow seems to remember. In fact, men seem to have a photographic memory of sins
against them. It can only be God's grace and mercy which makes
it so readily easy for Him to forgive. God not only has the ability
and nature to forgive, He also is able to forget. When God says He
doesn't remember our sins, then He does not remember them.

God causes Himself to forget, never remembering it again. When God does not remember something then HE has intentionally chosen to forget it. God somehow chooses to lose the remembrance of our sins and is able to completely lose the memory of them. It's a little funny God unable to find something. Our sins are never recalled to His recollection. God remembers not one single sin and that includes any you may have done today. God is able and willing to incur loss of the memory of it. He has the power to have no thought of it. Our sins are forever lost in God's forgetfulness. God has the loss of remembrance of our faults. It's the sweetest forgetfulness we will ever know. We can look to God as the Great Forgetter. Remember, sin is always broken fellowship with God which then means that the relationship needs to be restored. God chooses not to preserve the memory of our broken fellowship. His forgiveness excludes any idea of punishment or penalty imposed. Hallelujah, for God's short memory. However, God does remember our infirmities. Our infirmities are the needs and lack where we are destitute.

There are some things that we no longer remember. For example, there was a time when mom and dad changed our diapers and we were well aware of the fact, but we don't remember that anymore. In fact, we have totally forgotten that time. And if you do remember you were in them too long. Likewise we can forget things if we choose to. God loves us and will not carry our sins in His thoughts. How great and big is God's love.

Jesus Christ shed his blood for the remission of sins and his body was broken for our healing.

Luke 22:19 & 20

vs 19   And he took bread, and gave thanks, and brake *it*, and gave unto them, saying, This is my body which is given for you: this do in remembrance of me.

vs 20   Likewise also the cup after supper saying, This cup *is* the new testament in my blood, which is shed for you.

I Peter 2:24

Who [Jesus Christ] his own self bare our sins in his own body on the tree, that we, being dead to sins, should live unto righteousness, by whose stripes ye were healed.

It had always been God's will for His people to be forgiven and healed.

Psalm 103:3

Who [God] forgiveth all thine iniquities; who healeth all thy diseases;

You don't have any sin so big or so great that it is not or cannot be forgiven. That includes those same ones you continue to do over and over again. It's that sin nature we got from "the factory" the day we first drew breath. The Hebrew word for both "alls" in this verse is *kowl*. It means any or every, as many as. And it is ALL: ALL without exception. The verse says, "all iniquities, all diseases." You can't have too many sins. You cannot turn so black in your heart that God cannot wash away all the uncleanness in you. God has an unlimited amount of forgiveness. Of course, we don't want to *try* to use up all God's forgiveness because our rewards in heaven are based on how we walk with God in this life. We don't want to shortchange ourselves at heaven's door. Nevertheless, God will continue to forgive our sins and shortcomings over and over again because it is His nature. It is why He sent His only begotten son as our savior.

Just as God forgives all our iniquities and sins, he heals all our diseases and sicknesses. It's just as easy for God to deliver you from a cold as it is for Him to deliver you from the worst diseases known or unknown to mankind.

Did you ever wonder where sickness comes from? All sickness is a result of sin, directly or indirectly. When Adam and Eve committed the first sin, it started the corruption of the blood in mankind. Adam and Eve's flesh and blood were no longer perfect. As a result, they could become sick and eventually die. Adam and Eve were never sick before they sinned. As mankind continued to produce and sin multiplied, more and more genetic weaknesses increased and the gene pool became weaker. As a result mankind has more physical flaws and will continue to produce new sicknesses and diseases.

God is the only one who truly knows where our sickness comes from. For example, some families have particular weaknesses like genetic heart problems, high blood pressure or any number of diseases. You may wonder how far back in your genetic pool the body began to break down. Only God knows if what is making you sick is your sin or your great, great, great grandpappy's who was born in the late 1700's.

Never look with a critical eye at someone who has a sickness or disease, because you don't know where it came from. The sick and diseased are to be treated with kindness and tenderness. We are to walk in love, because it may very well, not be their fault. And that's a place we should prefer not to judge, and be wrong. Some gene pool's need a little "spiritual" bleach. They need the Word of God to clean things up. The more Word of God that we believe and do, the purer the blood. The more generations who believe, the better the blood will become. But what really matters is that God is the Great Healer of our diseases.

Whether you came from the "factory" with a physical problem or developed a problem later that originated in the past because of someone else's sin, you don't have to live with it. God can and will heal you if you go to His Word and believe the promise.

You know, if I have a sickness and it's the result of someone else's sin back in my family history, man I'm not living with that! We may not be able to change the past, but we can change what we believe in order to get deliverance and change our future. Many people in God's Word did it.

In my home, when one of us gets sick we look to God for healing. We have what we call first aid, second aid, and third aid. First aid is going to God directly first. We pray and ask God ourselves. We pour out our hearts to Him first. Then, if we don't receive our deliverance we move on to second aid. Second aid is being ministered to or prayed for by someone else. And third aid is if we still have not received our deliverance and our believing is not there, we go see the doc. And we certainly do not condemn ourselves for our inadequacies and lack of believing in this area of our lives.

All healing comes from God. Do you know why? It is because God made our bodies to heal. Think about it. When you cut yourself, you body immediately rushes antibodies and coagulants to the scene of the invasion to heal it. If your body didn't heal itself, you would simple die due to excessive bleeding or infection. But God, in His foreknowledge knew that we would need healing and provided it by designing our bodies to heal themselves.

I was up on a ladder one day while I was working. The ladder was leaning against the second story of a commercial building. Suddenly, the bottom of the ladder slid out and I slammed down onto the concrete. And I thank God it was second aid where my miracle of healing took place. I would have preferred healing when I went to God myself, but my believing was just not there. So I made a phone call and a friend prayed and ministered healing to me. I will always remember God's healing power of love as long as I live. And the other blessing was it didn't cost me a penny. It's always free medical when it comes from the hand of God. There are never any ill side effects or the worry of it ever coming back. By the way, when God heals something like a broken bone, when x-rayed later it would show no evidence of the break. Man cannot mend and heal like that. Man simple aides the body to heal itself. You cannot buy God's design of the body, it was free. No man can promise to heal you, only God can.

In the following record, Jesus Christ heals a man that was born blind.

John 9:1 – 7

vs 1   And as Jesus passed by, he saw a man which was blind from his birth.

vs 2   And his disciples asked him, saying, Master, who did sin, this man, or his parents, that he was born blind?

vs 3   Jesus answered, Neither hath this man sinned, nor his parents: but that the works of God should be made manifest in him.

His parents did nothing to cause this blindness in their son, and obviously the man could not have sinned since he was born blind. Neither does this mean God made this man blind from birth. In light of God's foreknowledge this verse makes more sense. God knew this man would believe for healing.

> vs 4   I must work the works of him that sent
> me, while it is day: the night cometh, when no
> man can work.

As long as the light is here, Jesus Christ is day. And now we are keeping the spiritual day shining. If Christ was spoken of nowhere, it would be spiritual night and darkness every where. People are either spreading darkness or light.

> vs 5   As long as I am in the world, I am the
> light of the world.

> vs 6   When he had thus spoken, he spat on
> the ground, and made clay of the spittle, and he
> anointed the eyes of the blind man with the clay,

In the Eastern culture people believed that spit of a holy man caused healing. This is what this man needed to build his confidence to the point of believing to receive his healing. It's amazing how the spirit of God can work within you. If we walked by revelation in situations we would see more miracles of healing.

God is just as willing to heal people today as He was then. He has not changed even a little. It's the temperature of believing and elevation of it that is the problem. We have to overcome the belief that we *can't*. We need to walk with God and allow the spirit of God to work within us. God wants us walking in word of knowledge, word of wisdom and discerning of spirits.

God communicates to the spirit He gave us, which is Christ in us. Then our spirit communicates to our mind, making things known to us which by our senses we would never know. It's that still small voice from God Himself. It's a voice that calms and stills the mind and heart. It's a tone that is distinct and clear. To me it has a pitch and tone to it that frees and sets the heart ablaze. It's sad to say that the hue and color of that voice sometimes changes when I screw up. Sometimes it has a slight reminder of my parents when I was growing up. However, when it is over, I know I have been loved.

> vs 7   And said [Jesus Christ] unto him, Go, wash in the pool of Siloam, (which is by interpretation, Sent.) He went his way therefore, and washed, and came seeing.

This was not an instantaneous miracle, because it happened over time. The man followed Christ's instructions and then came seeing. That was what was needed in order to bring this man to the point of believing. God knows what needs to be done to bring or get us to the place where we are able to believe. God knew exactly what this man needed, and what he needed to do to believe. When this man received his eyesight restored, he would not have needed glasses to read, he would have had perfect eye sight. His healing was complete.

God's healing is just as complete as His forgiveness.

Psalm 103:12

As far as the east is from the west, so far hath he removed our transgressions from us.

If you head east, you can go around the world as many times as you like and you will always be heading east. In the same way, if you go west, you will continue going west. However, it is not true if you head north or south. If you head north toward the north pole, eventually you will start heading south. Our sins have been removed a long way–as far as the east is from the west. The two will never meet. Our sins have been so removed from us that I can't really get my mind around it. When God forgives us, it is completely and thoroughly complete.

Forgiveness is a quality that we as Christians need to emulate. The problem is, it's usually easier to be on the receiving side than the giving side of forgiveness. But holding on to bitterness and resentment affects our minds and bodies which can cause sickness. Sickness in the mind will seep illness into the body. Look at what Jesus Christ said about loving your enemies.

Matthew 5:43 – 46

vs 43   Ye have heard that it hath been said, Thou shalt love thy neighbour, and hate thine enemy.

vs 44   But I say unto you, Love your enemies, bless them that curse you, do good to them that hate you, and pray for them which despitefully use you, and persecute you;

Forgiveness is good for the heart. To pray for people that hate you, that despitefully use you and that persecute you, does more for your physical and mental health and well being than you will ever know. There is healing in the act of forgiving itself. The act of forgiving does so much for our entire well being.

vs 45   That ye may be the children of your Father which is in heaven: for he maketh his sun to rise on the evil and on the good, and sendeth rain on the just and on the unjust.

vs 46   For if ye love them which love you, what reward have ye? do not even the publicans the same?

God shows his love to everyone irrespective if they are a Christian or unbeliever, a saint or a sinner, if they're just or unjust. God has the sun to shine on the evil and the good, and his rain falls on the just and unjust. God wants everyone to know they are loved by Him. The unchanging laws of God are His way of constantly showing His love and mercy to everyone. But, it is not just by nature that they see His love. They also see God's love in our lives. This is how a lot of us got born again. In Romans 2:4 it's the goodness of God that leadeth thee to repentance.

God loves the evil and unjust as much as He loves us. The rain falls on them the same as it does us. We are God's kids, God loves our enemies, how else will they be won. Children that are followers of God are to mimic Him, as kids do their parents. God does not have any hands but our hands to walk among the almost dead. The unjust see the love we have for God and one another. They must also see the love we have for them. It's God's love that drew us and it is God's love that will draw them. The love and forgiveness we have in our hearts is one of the major things the unsaved can see to become saved. It's a witness to the unjust.

John 13:35

By this shall all men know that ye are my disciples, if ye have love one to another.

We belong to God. We are His, and He is ours. The God rejecter or unbelievers belong to the devil. The adversary has legal rights over the unsaved. He has not even one right over the saved. However, the devil is constantly trying to afflict the believer, make him sick, poverty stricken, miserable and make him suffer in any area he can. God is always fighting for us and the devil is always fighting against us. If the devil could, he would stop the rain from falling on the just, and have it just fall on his people. Why would the devil want to hurt his own? A kingdom divided cannot stand. The devil wants the lost to have lots of money, live in good homes, have a good time, be healthy, and think life is great. After all it's his best shot at winning them and keeping them. God set life up where the unsaved can operate the law of believing the same as the saved. They can prosper the same as us.

The adversary wants to make the Christian look stupid and defeated in any way he can. And too often he does. We don't claim our rights in Christ, because half the time most Christians don't know them. The devil has no rights over you, so don't give him any. The devil will try to kick your tail any way he can. He will tell you, you have no right to health, prosperity and happiness. He will endeavor to rack and ruin your life – it's his nature.

The devil knows once you have the spirit of God in you, you have eternal life, and he knows he can't change that. That spirit is seed. God cannot and will not reverse that. That spirit within you, Christ in you, does not come and go irrespective of how good or bad you are. Once you are God's kid, no matter what you do that will never change. That started on the day of Pentecost.

1 Peter 1:23

Being born again, not of corruptible seed, but of
incorruptible, by the word of God, which liveth
and abideth for ever.

The devil wants to make the saved look defeated, make
them negative and miserable in every way he can. That is why
the wicked prosper. The devil lets their lives go on as uninter-
rupted as he can. He does not put road blocks up and no U-
turns for them. We must start to claim our rights, our legal rights
in Christ, that God has given us. We must view life in light of
the saying, "the future is as bright as the promises of God." How
can you claim promises you don't know? And how many are
we claiming of the ones we do know? God's Word has all the
answers and the solutions in life. The more abundant life is the
greatest life that can be lived. It's where the greatest amount of
peace and joyfulness come from.

We are sons of God, the Creator of the heavens and the
earth. We have sonship rights and privileges. Let's not allow the
adversary to talk us out of them. Even in the Word the godless
said and continue to say, "Why should we pray to your God?
We have everything we need." If the devil can make the god rejecter's life look better than God's kids life, he may succeed in
some not being won to Christ.

2 Corinthians 4:4

In whom the god of this world hath blinded the minds of them which believe not, lest the light of the glorious gospel of Christ, who is the image of God, should shine unto them.

He didn't blind our minds to the glorious gospel. Eternal life is the greatest thing I am thankful to God for. And hope is always something you anticipate and look forward to in the future. Hope always anticipates, and it's the anticipation that is keeping me waiting. Hope is one of the three greatest things you need in your life. Love and believing are the other two. We have the greatest hope to look forward to of all the people who walk the earth.

Recognize that you are forgiven by God and allow the healing balm of God's love to heal your mind and soul. Claim the promises of forgiveness and health because Jesus Christ sacrificed his life so that you could be free from condemnation and sickness. Depression and illness be gone in the powerful name of Jesus Christ. God's will is a peaceful mind and a healthy, painless body. We can believe God to stay healthy. The best time to heal an illness is before you get it. Preventative believing is a wonderful way to stay healthy. Our health is to be enjoyed and so is our forgiveness.

SPIRITUAL GOODIES
For Forgiveness and Health

- One thing God gives away more than anything else is forgiveness. It may be the only area that He would like to give less.

- How can we draw nigh to God if we think He is displeased or angry with us?

- My wife is always telling me she can explain it to me, but she doesn't know how yet to understand it for me.

- Forgiveness releases a weight and burden that opens the door for your heart to heal.

- Forgiving is some of the best giving you will ever do.

- Holding a grudge is taxing on your body. It causes headaches, sickness and is a miserable thing to live with.

- We sometimes need to forgive for the sake of our own sanity.

- There is great sorrow and pain in one who cannot forgive himself.

- The healing process begins when your forgiving begins.

- The easiest and clearest part of God's love to see is His daily forgiveness.

- The greatest freedom you will ever have in this life is when you know and believe you are forgiven by God Himself. And the truth of that is present daily.

- The less forgiveness shown, the more scarring of your own heart.

- When you pray for those who hurt you, you are well on way to being healed, or you may have already been healed.

- God is the sole Author and Originator of forgiveness. He was the first to give it and He will be the last to ever give it again.

- Remission of sins is a one-time event. It happens when you get born again. Remission happens when all your sin is forgiven at one time. It gets remitted. Forgiveness of sins is a continual thing. Some need more than others.

- It may be that more times than not, the person being forgiven did not even know they needed it. And in my marriage that's a shoe that fits me.

- We want an offence that we were a part of forgiven quickly and forgotten quicker.

- When I was younger, I had friend that I took too long to forgive and he moved on.

- When God proclaims He has forgiven us, then He has forgiven us.

- Believing is what makes the unseen visible.

- Your forgiveness of a debt or obligation can release someone from a promise they cannot keep.

- Eternal rewards are by merit, eternal life is not and neither is forgiveness.

- How many things have you released yourself from when you forgive? Things such as bitterness, self-pity, hurt, and the tendency to seek revenge. All these things will rack and ruin your life.

- A great barometer in knowing you have forgiven someone, you pray for them and wish the best for them.

- We don't like being around people we have not forgiven, or people who have not forgiven us.

- You can forgive because God forgave you first.

- The Word of God gives a person the power and freedom to forgive.

- When you forgive you grow.

- There is not a day that goes by that we don't need God's forgiveness.

- "Don't forget, I forgave you for that!" Don't hold your fictitious forgiveness over someone's head.

- There is a wonderful fulfillment and satisfaction when you know in your heart you are doing something for one of God's kids that accounts for something. And, that means more to God than you know.

Chapter Seven

Your Prayers To God

Prayer is a thing God made so we could fellowship with Him and live a more abundant life. Prayer is communion with God and sharing our heart with our Father. Prayer provides a unique relationship in our communication with God. It brings us closer to God and it builds a bond in a way in which were able to know Him better and grow into a greater understanding of Him. The Word of God does not say we have to pray to get born again, it says believe in your heart that God raised Christ from the dead and you will receive eternal life and become a son of God.

Prayer provides a deep personal fulfillment in the life of a man or woman. Prayer should be as common and familiar to us as our meals throughout the day. Faithful prayer on a regular basis can be one of the highlights of your life. It was for Jesus Christ and many others in God's Word. Prayer is to be enjoyed and ought to be some of the greatest times of our lives with God. It's a beautiful way of enjoying the presence of God. Prayer does not just change things around you, it changes you.

It changes you on the inside, which will change things on the outside. What's more powerful than prayer with believing? That is especially true when God has put something on your heart to believe for.

As a result of a vital prayer life, the bulk of life can be lived without a care in the world. We won't weary or worry ourselves half to death. God made life to be lived and enjoyed to the fullest.

1 Peter 5:7

Casting all your care upon him; for he careth
for you.

The word "care" in this verse is anxious care, thoughts that carry anxiety in and with them. They are thoughts that distract the mind and trouble it. God doesn't want us to carry anxiety around with us. That's some love when you don't want someone to carry baggage in their mind. And who knows the baggage that we cart around in our minds better than us? God wants us to give Him the anxious mental baggage because He cares for us. There is no one else you can give it to. No one else wants it or would take it from you. We all have more than we would like to admit. It does not have to be that way. Get busy casting, and don't let any of it trickle back in your heart. It's so freeing to give it to God. Who else can we so freely share our heart and thoughts with? God is someone we can completely be ourselves with.

James 4:8a

Draw nigh to God, and he will draw nigh to you.

God is always willing to draw close to us. Are we willing to draw close to Him? We draw near to God by doing His Word. What would get us nearer to God's heart than prayer? You have truly humbled yourself to God when you're praying to Him. Prayer between you and God is always to be honest and pure. Man cannot hide anything from God.

God is the only one we should pray to. Prayer and worship are the ultimate in commitment. When you pray, you are giving your life and soul to that which you pray to. The God that created the heavens and the earth, the God of my Lord and Savior Jesus Christ who gave me eternal life and made life where l can and will go live forever with them, that's the only God I am going to pray to or worship. The thought that a person would pray to something or worship something else is repugnant. Neither the devil nor anything in the world will ever get my prayers or worship. Only God has earned and deserves our prayer.

Jesus Christ's life was permeated with prayer. He had the prayer life to follow.

Matthew 14:23 – 32

vs 23   And when he had sent the multitudes away, he went up into a mountain apart to

pray: and when the evening was come, he was
there alone.

Some of our greatest times and moments with God are as
a result of prayer. Look what happens following this time of
prayer.

> vs 24   But the ship was now in the midst of the
> sea, tossed with waves: for the wind was con-
> trary.

> vs 25   And in the fourth watch of the night
> [between the hours of 3:00 a.m. and 6:00 a.m.]
> Jesus went unto them, walking on the sea.

> vs 26   And when the disciples saw him walk-
> ing on the sea, they were troubled, saying, It is a
> spirit; and they cried out for fear.

> vs 27   But straightway Jesus spake unto them,
> saying, Be of good cheer; it is I; be not afraid.

> vs 28   And Peter answered him and said, Lord, if
> it be thou, bid me come unto thee on the water.

> vs 29   And he said, Come. And when Peter was
> come down out of the ship, he walked on the
> water, to go to Jesus.

vs 30   But when he saw the wind boisterous,
[He walked by his senses instead of continuing
to look at the Lord. This was his failure and ours
also when we don't continue to stay focused on
the Lord.] he was afraid; and beginning to sink,
he cried, saying, Lord, save me.

vs 31   And immediately Jesus stretched forth
his hand, and caught him, and said unto him, O
thou of little faith, wherefore didst thou doubt?

vs 32   And when they were come into the ship,
the wind ceased.

Doubt is the biggest killer of prayer I know. Peter was walking on the water until he became afraid and doubted. Christ's believing inspired Peter's believing for a bit. You can so see Christ's heart of love to Peter, his encouragement to continue on when he said to him, "Wherefore didst thou doubt?" Can you picture his face and visage; like a mom or dad encouraging their baby in their first steps? Of course, God's Word doesn't describe Christ's visage, but we can be sure it was loving. Peter was outspoken and had some flaws. The rest of these guys on the boat must have been pretty inspired to see both Peter and Christ walking on the water. I sure would have loved to have been there. They would not have been the only ones having all the fun. Running on the water, grabbing someone's shirt tail and skiing behind them, what a day at the lake! Then imagine going to get something to eat with Christ. Then can't you see yourself lounging around listening to Christ teach you the Word? Put yourself into the records in God's Word. These are not just stories. These are records of history. Peter, James, John and the others were men just like us.

The following verses record Jesus Christ removing himself time and again to be alone to pray.

Mark 6:46

And when he had sent them away, he departed into a mountain to pray.

Luke 9:18

And it came to pass, as he was alone praying, his disciples were with him: and he asked them, saying, Whom say the people that I am?

In both records he was alone praying. Christ prayed alone often. It was common place for him to be alone and pray and talk to God. He spent time in prayer wanting to know and do God's will. Even though he was extremely busy, healing, teaching and serving God's people, he took time out to pray to his Father. We often have hectic, busy lives, but we cannot afford not to take time to be alone and pray.

Luke 6:12

And it came to pass in those days, that he went
out into a mountain to pray, and continued all
night in prayer to God.

I have tried a few times and found myself following the disciple's example. The spirit is willing but the flesh is weak. Remember God looks on the heart. No one has had the drive of love in their heart like Christ. Christ knew how to push himself mentally and physically like no other man who has ever lived. When he worked as a carpenter, he was the best carpenter there ever was. He would have had the ability to be anything he wanted to be. If he lived today, instead of being a carpenter he could have been a Navy SEAL. He would have broken all records and what a SEAL instructor he would make – no one would be able to keep up with him. Christ would leave them all in the dust. As amazing as the SEALS are today, they would be far better if Christ was their instructor. He would teach them about revelation from God. Then they would be able to hear from God what the enemy is going to do. How would you like to know that information going into battle? However, being a SEAL is not what he would do. All of Jesus Christ's heart, love and ability was focused on his relationship with God and being the savior of the world.

As we spend more and more time in prayer, we learn to believe and trust God more. Believing is what gives wings to our prayers.

Matthew 21:22

And all things, whatsoever ye shall ask in prayer,

believing, ye shall receive.

When you pray, believe you shall receive. You keep praying and believing until it comes to pass. God is fighting for us and the devil is fighting against us, but we determine the outcome. Like Peter who walked on the water, we need to overcome being afraid and eliminate our doubt.

I Samuel 12:23

Moreover as for me, God forbid that I should

sin against the LORD in ceasing to pray for you:

but I will teach you the good and the right way:

God calls it sin not to pray for others. It can be a sin that is easily overcome. Just pray for your friends and enemies. We're all going to sin and fall short. However, prayer does not have to be a category that we miss the mark. Remember prayer is to be enjoyed and cherished. Some of the greatest miracles in life come about by prayer.

Psalm 5:2

Hearken unto the voice of my cry, my King, and

my God: for unto thee will I pray.

Psalm 5:3

My voice shalt thou hear in the morning, O
LORD; in the morning will I direct my prayer
unto thee, and will look up.

David started his day with prayer. There's not a better way to start our day. It makes the whole day the best. I don't know where the idea comes from that it has to be some long drawn out prayer. Simply thank God for Him taking care of the things that are important to you: your wife, husband, kids, pets, friends, health, people you want to help and bless, the things you want to overcome and the things you want to accomplish. God hears and receives our prayers. Gee, I did put your pets before your friends, oh well they're sometimes easier to get along with.

At the end of verse three it says, " . . . and will look up." It means that David will watch and look for the answer from God. God answers prayer. When you pray keep looking for the answer.

In the Book of Isaiah, King Hezekiah prays unto the Lord with his heart.

Isaiah 38:1 – 5

vs 1   In those days was Hezekiah sick unto
death. And Isaiah the prophet the son of Amoz
came unto him, and said unto him, Thus saith
the LORD, Set thine house in order: for thou
shalt die, and not live.

> vs 2   Then Hezekiah turned his face toward
> the wall, and prayed unto the LORD,

> vs 3   And said, Remember now, O LORD, I
> beseech thee, how I have walked before thee in
> truth and with a perfect heart, and have done
> that which is good in thy sight. And Hezekiah
> wept sore.

Hezekiah walked in truth and spoke the truth about God's Word. His heart was perfect in his devotion to God. This was his prayer to God in regards to his life. Hezekiah's prayer inspires me to live like that.

> vs 4   Then came the word of the LORD to
> Isaiah, saying,

> vs 5   Go, and say to Hezekiah, Thus saith
> the LORD, the God of David thy father, I have
> heard thy prayer, I have seen thy tears: behold, I
> will add unto thy days fifteen years.

Uh prayer, how blessed would you be to pray and have fifteen more years added to your life when your time was up? No doctor could promise you that. God added the fifteen years to the King's life, but that wasn't all the Lord did.

vs 6   And I will deliver thee and this city out
of the hand of the king of Assyria: and I will
defend this city.

vs 7   And this shall be a sign unto thee from
the Lord, that the Lord will do this thing that he
hath spoken.

vs 8   Behold, I will bring again the shadow
of the degrees, which is gone down in the sun
dial of Ahaz, ten degrees backward. So the sun
returned ten degrees, by which degrees it was
gone down.

Hezekiah didn't ask for deliverance from the King of Assyria,
yet God granted it to him. Furthermore, the Lord wanted Hezekiah to have a powerful sign to know that He would do what He
said. In verse eight it says that the Lord would cause the sun to
turn back by ten degrees on the sun dial. Signs and wonders follow those who believe.

Mark 16:20

And they [the apostles] went forth, and
preached every where, the Lord working with
them, and confirming the word with signs following. Amen.

While Daniel is praying in this record, the angel Gabriel pays him a visit.

Daniel 9:20 – 22

vs 20   And whiles I was speaking, and praying, and confessing my sin and the sin of my people Israel, and presenting my supplication before the LORD my God for the holy mountain of my God;

vs 21   Yea, whiles I was speaking in prayer, even the man Gabriel [the angel Gabriel], whom I had seen in the vision at the beginning, being caused to fly swiftly, touched me about the time of the evening oblation [offering].

vs 22   And he informed me, and talked with me, and said, O Daniel, I am now come forth to give thee skill and understanding.

People's prayers change their lives. We could all use some more skill and understanding. And this kind of understanding is far off the beaten path.

Here's another record of healing deliverance as a result of prayer.

I Kings 13:6

And the king [Jeroboam] answered and said
unto the man of God, Intreat now the face of the
LORD thy God, and pray for me, that my hand
may be restored me again. And the man of God
besought the LORD, and the king's hand was
restored him again, and became as it was before.

There is physical healing in prayer. We can pray for people and if they believe, they can be healed. Jeroboam was not a good king, so it was not his goodness that healed him. He believed and received his healing. God blesses you according to your believing, not how good you are. I assure you; we will never become good enough to receive from God. You will never read in the scriptures where God says, "When you're good enough, I will bless you." That's something we can all be thankful for.

Praying for others should be a big part of our prayer life.

Matthew 5:44

But I say unto you, Love your enemies, bless
them that curse you, do good to them that hate
you, and pray for them which despitefully use
you, and persecute you.

If you can live this verse with the right heart you're the best. It may be one of the most difficult verses to live. However, if it were not possible to do it, God would not have put it in his Word. Sometimes I live this verse, sometimes not. It is amazing the freeness it gives and brings when it is lived.

In the Old Testament there was a woman named Hannah. She greatly wanted a child. It was a great need in her life. She prayed unto the Lord.

I Samuel 1:10 & 11, 25b, 26 – 28

vs 10   And she was in bitterness of soul, and prayed unto the Lord, and wept sore.

vs 11   And she vowed a vow, and said, O Lord of hosts, if thou wilt indeed look on the affliction of thine handmaid, and remember me, and not forget thine handmaid, but wilt give unto thine handmaid a man child, then I will give him unto the Lord all the days of his life, and there shall no razor come upon his head ["no razor come upon his head" indicates a special commitment to serve God].

God answered her prayer and gave her a son. Hannah prayed for a child and was blessed with Samuel. All the barren women in the Word that prayed and believed God, had sons. When he was older, Hannah brought Samuel to the temple to serve the Lord as she vowed.

vs 25b and brought the child to Eli.

vs 26   And she said, Oh my lord, as thy soul
liveth, my lord, I am the woman that stood by
thee here, praying unto the LORD.

vs 27   For this child I prayed; and the LORD
hath given me my petition which I asked of him:

Hannah and her husband Elkanah visited Samuel on a yearly
basis. During one of their visits look at what God did for this
wonderful husband and wife.

I Samuel 2:20 & 21

And Eli blessed Elkanah and his wife, and said,
The Lord give thee seed of this woman for the
loan which is lent to the Lord. And they went
unto their own home.

And the Lord visited Hannah, so that she conceived, and
bare three sons and two daughters. And the child Samuel grew
before the Lord.

Hannah prayed for one child and promised to lend him to
the Lord. God in turn blesses her with four sons and two daughters. Talk about answer to prayer!

For years the doctors told my wife and I that we could not
have children. I was younger when the doctors told us this and I

had the energy of my conviction. But, this will be a good Christian book and some things will be better left unsaid. God said we are to be fruitful and multiply. We made up our minds to believe what God's Word said and we were not going to be told we could not do the will of God in our lives. It's a wonderful thing for a wife and husband to pray together. We named our son Samuel after Hannah's son. Samuel means "asked of God." We asked of God and He heard our prayer.

Matthew 18:19

Again I say unto you, That if two of you shall agree on earth as touching any thing that they shall ask, it shall be done for them of my Father which is in heaven.

Daniel had a strong prayer life. Prayer takes commitment of the heart.

Daniel 6:7 – 23

vs 7   All the presidents of the kingdom, the governors, and the princes, the counsellors, and the captains, have consulted together to establish a royal statute, and to make a firm decree, that whosoever shall ask a petition of any God or man for thirty days, save of thee, O king, he shall be cast into the den of lions.

vs 8   Now, O king, establish the decree, and sign the writing, that it be not changed, according to the law of the Medes and Persians, which altereth not.

vs 9   Wherefore king Darius signed the writing and the decree.

vs 10   Now when Daniel knew that the writing was signed, he went into his house; and his windows being open in his chamber toward Jerusalem, he kneeled upon his knees three times a day, and prayed, and gave thanks before his God, as he did aforetime.

vs 11   Then these men assembled, and found Daniel praying and making supplication before his God.

vs 12   Then they came near, and spake before the king concerning the king's decree; Hast thou not signed a decree, that every man that shall ask a petition of any God or man within thirty days, save of thee, O king, shall be cast into the den of lions? The king answered and said, The thing is true, according to the law of the Medes and Persians, which altereth not.

vs 13   Then answered they and said before the king, That Daniel, which is of the children of the captivity of Judah, regardeth not thee, O king, nor the decree that thou hast signed, but maketh his petition three times a day.

vs 14   Then the king, when he heard these words, was sore displeased with himself, and set his heart on Daniel to deliver him: and he laboured till the going down of the sun to deliver him.

vs 15   Then these men assembled unto the king, and said unto the king, Know, O king, that the law of the Medes and Persians is, That no decree nor statute which the king establisheth may be changed.

vs 16   Then the king commanded, and they brought Daniel, and cast him into the den of lions. Now the king spake and said unto Daniel, Thy God whom thou servest continually, he will deliver thee.

vs 17   And a stone was brought, and laid upon the mouth of the den; and the king sealed it with his own signet, and with the signet of his lords; that the purpose might not be changed concerning Daniel.

vs 18   Then the king went to his palace, and passed the night fasting: neither were instruments of musick brought before him: and his sleep went from him. [This king had some heart]

vs 19   Then the king arose very early in the morning, and went in haste unto the den of lions.

vs 20   And when he came to the den, he cried with a lamentable voice unto Daniel: and the king spake and said to Daniel, O Daniel, servant of the living God, is thy God, whom thou servest continually, able to deliver thee from the lions?

vs 21   Then said Daniel unto the king, O king, live for ever.

vs 22   My God hath sent his angel, and hath shut the lions' mouths, that they have not hurt me: forasmuch as before him innocency was found in me; and also before thee, O king, have I done no hurt.

vs 23   Then was the king exceeding glad for him, and commanded that they should take Daniel up out of the den. So Daniel was taken up out of the den, and no manner of hurt was found upon him, because he believed in his God.

Daniel prayed three times a day. Biblically, the number three means complete. The people you read about in God's Word all had prayer in common. Prayer serving for the use of all. When Christ prayed it was a two way communication. God does not leave his people hanging. God conversed with His people when they prayed. These people viewed prayer as something precious and rare. Prayer carried value to them in their hearts and lives. Prayer is a priceless thing to learn and do. These people asked and let their requests be made known to God. In prayer a lot of the variables that God does go unnoticed. What they prayed for came into concretion in their lives.

It's not a church if it's not a house of prayer. God wants our hearts to be open to Him and our discourse free in our prayers to Him. The people you read about in God's Word had such an open heartedness and conversed so freely with God. If you beg in prayer, you will deprive yourself. To resort or stoop to beggary is a big sign of resorting to fear which is unbelief. Pray often. Praying frequently is one of the greatest principles of killing unbelief and building positive believing to receiving answers to your prayer.

Ruth Graham said, "Just pray for a tough hide and a tender heart." Ruth wrote me a letter which I keep it in my bible because I get blessed to read it from time to time. Ruth closed her letter to me with these words, "May God bless you and your efforts to enlighten and equip His people. May He open doors for you to get His Word out." That's what the apostle Paul prayed for the people.

SPIRITUAL GOODIES
For Your Prayers to God

- Most of the greatest miracles in life come as a result of prayer.

- Beggary in prayer is just another form of unbelief.

- Lack of prayer stunts every area of our spiritual growth.

- In prayer you are calling God to your aid. There is no one better to have in your corner.

- It's not a church if it's not a house of prayer.

- John Wesley said, "God does nothing except in response to believing prayer."

- Lack of prayer in your life is like heading into the desert with lack of water.

- When you send your prayer to God's throne, His act in return comes riding back on your believing.

- Prayer provides a unique way of knowing God that no other way supplies.

- Prayer is sharing your heart with God in an intimate fellowship with Him.

- You will never really know God if you don't pray often to Him.

- Prayer is a belief that you make a difference in the lives of others.

- Faithful prayer will help you look to God.

- Praying for someone IS making a difference in their life. It also makes a difference in the life of the person doing the praying.

- Prayer is the wood that keeps the fire of your believing hot.

- Of all the things we do that build believing in God's Word, prayer will rival them all.

- You will never know the value of a faithful prayer life until you have one.

- A minute or two every day in prayer can change your life.

- There are a lot of ways in life to get your needs met. The most neglected one is prayer, the other one is giving and receiving.

- Prayer is the building block of believing.

- Prayer stands by itself in accelerating believing. It determines how far and how fast you will go with God.

- Health and food are to be enjoyed; faithful prayer will be enjoyed more.

- The most hidden and selfless love you can show for someone is prayer.

- There are times when only prayer will bring deliverance.

- When we pray, we believe God hears our prayer. We must also believe He will answer it.

- That you would pray to God and worship Him is the ultimate in respect and reverence.

- Prayer is the ultimate in worship to God. In light of worship there is nothing that will surpass prayer.

- You will never rise above your prayer life.

Chapter Eight
The Forgiving Father

I can't think of anything more freeing to the heart and soul of a man or woman than knowing God has pardoned and remitted all their sins, and will continue His unconditional love of forgiveness toward His people. God is always ready and willing to offer forgiveness to His people. God by way of Jesus Christ gave us a full pardon. Complete forgiveness in all its pureness and holiness only comes from God. The forgiveness to obtain eternal life is only given by God Himself. Man can offer forgiveness one toward another, but only God can give eternal life forgiveness, which man receives when he gets born again. Forgiveness is very uplifting and healing to the soul. It's like the sin is just sent far away. We are offenders dealt with by God as not guilty, with no thought of punishment by God. The more I learn about forgiveness the greater I see that it's the truth that makes you free. It's a freedom only forgiveness releases. Forgiveness unshackles the pain and the restraints that imprison the heart. Bitterness, anger, wrath and revenge that torment and afflict the soul are released when you receive and give forgiveness. The release and freedom that forgiveness gives birth to, is healing. And we need not carry the load and burden of sin that sickens the soul any longer.

The cargos of suffering will accompany an unforgiving heart. No one freely gives forgiveness like God. However, if someone loves with the love of God, they will always find a way in their heart to pardon. Love is the main ingredient in forgiveness. Wherever forgiveness is, love and heart are always riding along with it. Love is the wheels that forgiveness comes on. To have a forgiving heart is very healing to the soul. We all have a need in our hearts to be forgiven, and to forgive.

Psalm 25:18

Look upon mine affliction and my pain; and
forgive all my sins.

It's often the guilt we carry from our sin that causes our affliction and pain. Thank God for your forgiveness, don't wallow in it. Immersing ourselves in guilt may be the most self-defeating thing we do. Jesus Christ often said to people, "Go in peace." It's the peace of God that is to rule in our hearts. We must root out the guilt and shame which causes the heart to suffer.

Matthew 26:28

For this is my blood of the new testament,
which is shed for many for the remission of sins.

The difference between remission of sins and forgiveness of sins is remission is a one-time occurrence. Jesus Christ's blood had to be shed so we could receive remission of sins. You receive remission of all your sins when you get born again. From that point on it's always forgiveness of sins. Sin is always broken fellowship with God. When we go to God and receive forgiveness from Him, we then have our fellowship with Him restored.

In Luke , chapter fifteen Jesus Christ tells the story of the forgiving father that had two sons.

Luke 15:11 & 1 2

vs 11   And he said, A certain man had two sons:

vs 12   And the younger of them said to his father, Father, give me the portion of goods that falleth to me. And he divided unto them his living.

The father gave both sons their portion. Both sons held in their hands their inheritance. They now have the choice to do with it what they will. They have freedom of will. God gave us all freedom of will to live for Him, or do whatever we want to do.

It's interesting that the younger son is the one who asks for his inheritance. God's Word mentions youthful lusts.

II Timothy 2:22

Flee also youthful lusts: but follow righteousness, faith, charity, peace, with them that call on the Lord out of a pure heart.

Luke 15:13 - 32

vs 13   And not many days after the younger son gathered all together, and took his journey into a far country, and there wasted his substance with riotous living.

vs 14   And when he had spent all, [Seems like we've all done this.] there arose a mighty famine in that land; and he began to be in want.

vs 15   And he went and joined himself to a citizen of that country; and he sent him into his fields to feed swine.

vs 16   And he would fain have filled his belly with the husks [pods of the carob tree] that the swine did eat: and no man gave unto him.

The world could care less about one of God's kids, even when you are starving to death. This would be especially true if there were a famine in the land, and you're in some foreign place where no one really knows you. The thought of eating what the pigs are eating, so we don't starve to death, might wake us up too. Then the son remembers how his father treats his servants.

> vs 17   And when he came to himself, [thought about his Father again] he said, How many hired servants of my father's have bread enough and to spare, [more than they can eat] and I perish with hunger!

This parable has a two-fold meaning. First, Jesus Christ is teaching about the relationship between a father and his son, but the greater truth is that he is teaching about the relationship between our Father and His children. Christ is teaching his disciples about fellowship with God. He is showing them that when we walk away from God, we spiritually die in our walk with God. If we stay away from God, God is left with staying away from us. We are not to remain in a condition that is away from God. That is not the will of God. God does not want us apart and distant from Him. It is the inactivity of our relationship with Him which causes unneeded pain and sorrow. When this happens, we end up living our lives the same way that the world does. We end up not really have anything to do with God. So those who are God's kids, have no fellowship or spiritual relationship with Him. We are still God's kids, but have no relationship with Him. The great truth of this record teaches that our spiritual relationship with God "perishes" when we walk away from Him and what we are to do to restore the broken fellowship.

> vs 18   I will arise and go to my father, and will
> say unto him, Father, I have sinned [broken fel-
> lowship] against heaven, and before thee,

To realize that you have sinned is the first step to getting back in fellowship. The son decides to go back to his father and confess his sins. Likewise, if we confess our sins [broken fellowship] He [God] is faithful and just to forgive us our sins. We go to God with an open and honest heart. This son woke up spiritually. God always looks on the heart. And this son saw he was dying spiritually, and wanted to start living again. People want to follow someone who won't let them down. In the Book of Ephesians we are to be followers of God.

> vs 19   And am no more worthy to be called thy
> son: make me as one of thy hired servants.

The son called himself "no more worthy." Somehow, some way we always want to condemn, and find self-reproach, after we have screwed up. We think we are no good , and must reprove ourselves, vigorously. We are then reprimanded by our own conscience, by our sense of guilt. It's no less important to forgive yourself, as it is to know you are forgiven. We seem to lose our sense of worth, to everybody, but mostly to our own selves and God. I even have a list I go through when I bottom out. I say to myself, "This vile body, just a clay pot, an old earthen vessel, body of sin, earthly house, my corrupt body, just a stranger and alien, a sojourner here in this life – this is what I am." Thank God, from time to time I just mentally visit this place. All the things I call myself in those times are in God's Word you know, however they are written with a little different heart than I just gave them. God never wants us to condemn ourselves. We never have to visit this place of despair.

> vs 20   And he arose, and came to his father. But
> when he was yet a great way off, his father saw
> him, and had compassion, and ran, and fell on
> his neck, and kissed him.

As Jesus Christ illustrates with the father in this record, God is waiting and looking for us all the time. It's as though the act had already been forgiven as soon as it started. This forgiveness is a forgetfulness that follows like a shadow. God welcomes us back with open arms and a loving embrace. God is always waiting and willing. If we will allow Him to heal us, we will rarely remember it happened. And when we do, it has very little effect on us. God is the healer of broken hearts. And He will mend the pieces of our hearts together again.

I wonder what was going on in the son's heart when he saw his father lovingly running to greet him. How would you have felt? God is opening His heart to us and showing us how He is to His children. Furthermore, if you have ears to hear you can see that Jesus Christ is teaching how moms and dads and brothers and sisters are to be with each other. The more love you have in your hearts, the easier it is.

> vs 21   And the son said unto him, Father, I
> have sinned against heaven, and in thy sight, and
> am no more worthy to be called thy son.

The son says again, "I no longer deserve to be called thy son." It's like a record that keeps skipping.

> vs 22   But the father said to his servants, Bring
> forth the best robe, and put it on him; and put a
> ring on his hand, and shoes on his feet:

The father completely and thoroughly ignores the statement of unworthiness that his son makes. He doesn't even address the remark, just like the verse that says God remembers our sins no more. The first thing He does is let him know he is loved. The father brought out the best robe. He was waiting for him all right. The father sends for the best clothes to help him start feeling better about himself. You feel good about yourself in great clothes, and these were the best. The ring is beautiful; it's a signet-ring. The ring gave the son the authority to use it over all matters of his father's property and business. It was used to stamp documents and other legal articles. No document was considered legal unless stamped by the ring. The sandals mark a free man. Servants went barefoot. Remember that the real Father in this section is God. This record is about love, forgiveness and fellowship with God, our heavenly Father.

> vs 23   And bring hither the fatted calf, and kill
> it; and let us eat, and be merry:

Imagine how hungry the son was. He had been eating carob pods that were meant for pigs. He was barely subsisting. He was about to perish. He probably thought, "I was hoping you would get to the food soon dad I am famished."

> vs 24   For this my son was dead, and is alive
> again; he was lost, and is found. And they began
> to be merry.

Spiritually, their relationship had no life. Now, the son is spiritually alive and in fellowship with his father again. When we return unto God, we are spiritually alive and living again and in fellowship with Him. How often we lose our way in life. Don't ever give up on your kids. They are not as far away as we think they might be at times. Just make sure they are not getting any food where they're at, they'll come back around.

> vs 25   Now his elder son was in the field: and as he came and drew nigh to the house, he heard musick and dancing.

> vs 26   And he called one of the servants, and asked what these things meant.

> vs 27   And he said unto him, Thy brother is come; and thy father hath killed the fatted calf, because he hath received him safe and sound.

God likes parties of this nature. The servant said "thy brother," reminding the older son of his relationship to the lost son. The servant was a good servant.

> vs 28   And he [the brother] was angry, and would not go in: therefore came his father out, and intreated [To call to one's side, to produce an effect, to exhort, help, comfort.] him.

God loves and helps all His kids regardless of how we are. Some may look good on the outside, but there is no one that does not need help on the inside. Why do we often work on the outside instead of cleaning up the inside? At times if we were to walk in someone else's shoes it might cause us to stumble too.

vs 29   And he answering said to his father,
Lo, these many years do I serve thee, neither
transgressed I at any time thy commandment:
and yet thou never gavest me a kid, that I might
make merry with my friends:

vs 30   But as soon as this thy son [thy son, not
my bother] was come, which hath devoured
thy [your money] living with harlots, thou hast
killed for him the fatted calf.

vs 31   And he said unto him, Son, [reminding
him of who his Father is lest he stumble too.]
thou art ever with me, and all that I have is thine.

This is always God's plea and cry to His people. We all have
access to all that is available from God, physically, mentally and
spiritually. God has given us all signet rings and shoes to wear.
All that God has is ours.

vs 32   It was meet that we should make merry,
and be glad: for this thy brother was dead, and is
alive again; and was lost, and is found.

The father refers to him as thy brother, not my son. When
anyone comes back to the family we should welcome them with
open arms, whether it's our brother or sister or mom or dad. It's

the right and loving thing to do. God just showed us the heart that we should have. There is a forgiveness that only God Himself can give: the forgiveness you received when you obtained eternal life. It is eternal life forgiveness. God's love and forgiveness are given unconditionally to all of us, irrespective of how good or bad we are. Some of us have been lost and found a few times in life. Let's all remember and live God's heart on the matter. We have forgiveness with Him and we are to forgive one another. What a big heart of love and forgiveness our Father has for His children.

SPIRITUAL GOODIES
For The Forgiving Father

- One thing that Christ never struggled with was sin-consciousness.

- God's the best company you will ever keep.

- When I blow it and do something stupid, asking God for forgiveness helps clear my sin-consciousness quicker than anything else.

- Keep the tail of your heart wagging and your soul purring with God.

- God loves you the same as He does Christ. We know God loves Christ. And He loves us the same.

- Always be honest with God. Any other way will rat you out.

- Thank God I didn't live in the Old Testament; I fear I may have been stoned many times over.

- Every day orphans find a Dad.

- Sin is man's greatest captivity. It's the one thing that drives us from God. Sin is broken fellowship with God.

- I enjoy hanging out with sinners, I can't find anybody else.

- Forgiveness is everything God claims it to be.

- Forgiveness is something you ask God for.

- The most healing thing in my life is knowing I have God's forgiveness every day.

Ephesians 4:31 & 32

Let all bitterness, and wrath, and anger, and clamour, and evil speaking, be put away from you, with all malice:

And be ye kind one to another, tenderhearted, forgiving one another, even as God for Christ's sake hath forgiven you.

- Put away all bitterness. We are not to harbor any venom or malice in our hearts of any kind.

- Kindness and forgiveness are languages that the deaf can hear, the blind can see and the mute can speak.

- I will forgive others as close as I can to the way God has forgiven me.

- Don't wait for someone to ask you for forgiveness. It will heal and bless their heart more if you freely give forgiveness with no strings attached.

- The greatest blessing in life is the conviction in your soul that you are loved by God unconditionally.

- When you forgive from the heart, it releases you from reliving the incident over and over again. Remembering it instead of forgiving it is like a record with the scratch on it that keeps playing that same beat over and over. The heartache and time in life wasted here is sorrow upon sorrow.

- Life is spiritual and short; don't hang that grudge in your heart like a coat on a hook.

- The greatest peace I have is the result of God's forgiveness that I have enjoyed.

- Your fellowship with God is deterred by your unwillingness to forgive.

- The healing and freedom forgiveness gives is not only to the forgiven but to the forgiver as well.

- It warms and melts God's heart when we ask for forgiveness.

- God is not angry or fierce with us when we make a mistake.

- That chip you are carrying on your shoulder will soon become a log.

- There are emotions tied to forgiveness and they are the kind that make you feel good.

- When you find it difficult to forgive someone, just remember what God has forgiven you for and what forgiveness you will need in the future.

- There is a wonderful forgetfulness in forgiving.

- There is more captivity and damage caused to our souls than we realize, when we recall to our minds the sins of the past that were not forgiven, whether ours or others.

- We need to be loved the most when we deserve to be loved the least.

- A grudge keeps the pilot light of revenge burning.

- God has an infinite capacity to forgive His kids and extend them mercy.

- There are spiritual heights that God longs for His people to reach and our spiritual growth and our spiritual survival depends on it.

Isaiah 40:31

But they that wait upon the LORD shall renew
their strength; they shall mount up with wings
as eagles; they shall run, and not be weary; and
they shall walk, and not faint.

- The eagle goes after its prey because its survival depends on it.

- Of all the sins I have seen in life, the most tormenting have been my own.

Chapter Nine
Believing Ye Shall Receive

There are two people that are both right: the man who says, "I can't" and the man who says, "I can." The law of believing governs a person's life more than anything else. What we believe is the very reason we are at where we're at today. And we will go tomorrow wherever our believing thoughts take us. There is nothing better a person can do than fill his or her mind with the positives of God's Word and live them. God's Word, in itself, is the most uplifting and edifying thing in life. There is no comparison to God's Word when it comes to something to believe in. As far as the east is from the west, that's the amount of hope that is in God's Word. God offers the greatest thing to believe in, bar none. What man offers pales in comparison to what God promises in His Word. The brightest future you could ever have is the one that trusts God and believes Him. Believing is so powerful it can help you conquer anything. It's the door to no failure for you. God's Word is the only place in the world where you will find perfect, unconditional love. Only God's love is unconditional love. You certainly will not find that in the world.

Worry and fear are contrary to God's Word. They have leeched and sucked more joy and happiness out of God's people than anything else. Worry leads to fear. Fear IS believing. It is just believing in reverse. Fear can bring massive mental fatigue to the heart and mind. Fear breeds more fear. Fear causes unbelief. Fear is contagious and spreads rapidly and quickly. Fear brings failure to our lives. Fear and unbelief have ruined more people than anything I know.

However, we do not need to have fear in our lives. God has helped so many of His people overcome fear of so many different things. God has helped me overcome mine. We can either choose to believe God or have fear in our lives which is the opposite of believing God. It's in believing what God says that we are able to overcome our worry and fear. As life goes by, new fears pop up. Don't let them snowball. Choose to believe God's promises each day anew. Handle each fear one by one as they come along by reading and believing what God's Word says. It's Christ in you who is superior to any circumstance you will ever face.

Matthew 21:22

And all things, whatsoever ye shall ask in prayer, believing, ye shall receive.

God has given us permission and allowed us to pray, believe and receive. No one has ever given you an invitational promise like that. It's a right that we have as sons and daughters of God. He has given us this right. Most people in the world don't have this sonship right or privilege because they are not God's children. You become a son or daughter of God by believing in the resurrection of Jesus Christ. God's Word is so clear and plain as to leave no doubt. If you're willing, God will help you become fully persuaded. Jesus Christ gives more authority and testimony to the Word of God than any one. He stands alone in giving proof and evidence to God's Word and that God is living and real.

Psalm 27:13

I had fainted, unless I had believed to see the
goodness of the LORD in the land of the living.

David's life was a witness to other people. He was persuaded to the end he had certainty that God would do what He said. God calls us believers because that's what He wants us to be. God's goodness is all that God has and wants to bless you with. God said in His Word that David believed to see the goodness of God in a land where people were living.

According to the Gallup Poll approximately seventy-five percent of Americans are Christians. In 1948, according to the first Gallup Poll, ninety-one percent of Americans were Christians.

Based on these percentages, if you go back to the year 1900, approximately ninety-seven percent of Americans may have been Christians. Let's believe God to see His goodness where we live.

Habakkuk 2:4b

. . . but the just shall live by his faith.

You have not lived until you are living this verse. If you want to live life to the fullest, there is no greater way to live it. The word "live" is the Hebrew word *chayah*: it means to have life, to live prosperously and flourish, to have health, to live without sickness, discouragement, to refresh, it also means to live forever. Anyone who believes in Jesus Christ and that God raised him from the dead has eternal life from God Himself and will live forever. Tell me a greater thought or truth that would bless you more than living with God and your family forever and ever, Amen. The verse says you live by your believing, not someone else's. You learn to really live life to the fullest by believing God.

Proverbs 23:7

For as he thinketh in his heart, so is he:

As you think, you are. We have to get rid of the thinking that we "can't" and replace it with the "I can do" attitude. We have to replace the old thoughts with new thoughts. We have to focus and stay focused on the light and promises of God's Word, because light is the only thing that dispels darkness. It's the Word that will help you get rid of the old dark belief that you can't. Have a goal, a dream with God – something you want to do for Him and let it have the highest priority in your heart. Then allow the time for it to come to pass. Sometimes in your walk with God, when you endeavor to accomplish great achievements, it requires time. It required time for Jesus Christ to be the savior of the world.

Philippians 4:13

I can do all things through Christ which strengtheneth me.

Now if you allow your mind to slip back into your old way of thinking, your old thought patterns, nothing is going to change. Everything in your life will remain the same or become worse. Far too often, we allow our emotions to influence our thinking. You have to continue to put on the Word in order to change. You have to put the new on in order to change the old way of thinking. You have to control your mind and thoughts. You can't do this for just a day or a few weeks. These thoughts have to become just as familiar to you and a part of you as the old way you thought, to the end it becomes the new you. The Word has a massive amount of power to heal the mind. There is great power in a believing mind of prayer. With God you can do anything.

Ephesians 4:22 – 24

vs 22   That ye put off concerning the former
conversation the old man, which is corrupt according to the deceitful lusts;

Our old nature is a slave to sin. The "old man" is as old as the
man himself. The "old man" is a figure of speech, meaning the
old way a person lived before getting born again. You put off the
old man by putting on the new man. That is what it means to
renew our minds to God's Word. Our old man didn't believe in
God worth a hoot. We are to dump those carnal worldly desires
with all their vanity, fear and unbelief. The world is full of syn-
thetic love and fairytale happiness. That is the old defeated way
of thinking. God's Word is full of His love and promises. We are
only limited by our lack of believing.

vs 23   And be renewed in the spirit [life] of
your mind;

This verse implies that the whole course of life will flow in a
different direction when we allow the Word to change our thinking. We can hear from God everyday in His Word. We are to also
hear from God by revelation. It's a conviction and truth in God's
Word which I cherish.

vs 24   And that ye put on the new man, [the

new nature] which after God is created in righteousness and true holiness.

The old man trusts God little if any. The new man is the one
that God is able to work with and help. The new man, your new
man, allows you and God to do something together. The only
way the old man will change is if you put on the new man. If you
don't put on the new man, the old man just gets worse. We must
read the Word, hear the Word and live the Word in order to get
rid of the old nature. We need God, His Word and His people to
convince us that we are not as bad as we think we are.

Proverbs 30:9

Lest I be full, and deny thee, and say, Who is the
Lord? Or lest I be poor, and steal, and take the
name of my God in vain.

The old man walks by his senses and views nothing spiritually. He has little or no respect for God or His Word. He's all
about self and very little about others. You have to get enough
Word in your heart and mind to change your thinking. You put
the new man on by putting on the Word of God. The old man
dies as you put on the new man. Those old fears and thoughts we
hate to think fall off. Who likes to have negative thoughts about
themselves? Who wants thoughts of weakness and failure? Who
wants to believe things like, "I'll never do that."? The old man is

our old nature, our former manner of living. Don't allow the old nature to influence your new believing. If we don't overcome our old man nature, our old man nature is sure to stop us from believing God. It's God's Word that inspires us to believe. We all want to aspire to something. God via His Word wants to help you. You are the only one who holds you back.

We have all lived the first part of the following verse more often than we would like to admit.

Proverbs 29:25

The fear of man bringeth a snare: but whoso putteth his trust in the LORD shall be safe.

When we don't put our trust in God this is what happens. Fear alw ays ensnares a person. It always binds your hands and thoughts. It's this fear of failure that we must overcome in order to achieve. I am an eye witness of my own self in the mirror that fear makes failures and cowards of us all. One thing I am not going to do when I'm older is look back with regrets of what was really important to me that I did not accomplish.

For example, fear has caused me not to do some of the things I wanted to do in my life. When I was young, you could never have convinced me that I would write a book. Fear enslaved me and made me think less of myself. When I was growing up, if the school I went to had a list for people who would not write a book, and more so a Christian book, my name would have been the first two names on the list. I believe writing this book is the will of God. I would not have believed that if God's Word had not helped me overcome my fear. However, the fact that you're reading this book is the result of my not allowing fear to win.

You have to picture what you want to come to pass in your mind before it will come to pass. And it needs to be the spirit of God at work within you, because we all know what it's like to try to do something yourself without God's help. There is nothing like God helping you achieve your goal and desire. You have to ask yourself if what you are doing brings glory to God, blesses God's people and blesses you as well. Nothing will satisfy or fulfill like doing the Word of God in your life. The reason I'm sharing this is to show you that anyone who hears enough Word of God, can have their believing built to the end that they will overcome and be victorious. Just for fun I should send a copy of this book to some of my old man friends from when I was growing up.

Before I received enough Word of God, fear defeated me at every turn. When I was young, I hated work with a passion. It was a four letter word not to be used or lived. That's why I had so many different jobs. From the age of nineteen to twenty-one I had twenty-two jobs in a twenty-four month period. At the time, variety was not the spice of life for me. I've had the same job now for over thirty years and that's not the spice of life either. Work is to be enjoyed and I thank God I enjoy work. My old man hated work, but the new man loves to work. A renewed mind will enjoy life in every capacity including work.

Job 3:25

For the thing which I greatly feared is come upon me, and that which I was afraid of is come unto me.

Who wants to experience this verse? If you fear something enough you can bet it will happen. If you are afraid of losing your job, you will lose it. Now fear is not something you doubt or worry about from time to time. This fear I'm referring to is a fear that you act upon consistently. It is the type of fear that controls areas of your life. In the book of Job God shows us the why of what happened to Job.

Job 1:5

And it was so, when the days of their feasting were gone about, that Job sent and sanctified them, and rose up early in the morning, and offered burnt offerings according to the number of them all: for Job said, It may be that my sons have sinned, and cursed God in their hearts. Thus did Job continually.

Job had a deep seeded fear that his kids had cursed God in their hearts. Because of this fear, he was making burnt offerings according to the number of them all. Fear, if not handled, will make a person do a lot of things that they would never do. Fear racks and ruins a believer's life more than any other single thing. It's a real enemy to a Christian. Fear in the believer's mind causes just the opposite of what he wants to happen. Fear erodes and eats away believing. Jesus Christ never feared or succumbed to any fear. Words like maybe, could be, if you're lucky, and I'm afraid were not in Christ's thinking or his vocabulary.

Fear can be a cage, the bars that hold you back from being everything that God would have you to be and everything that you want to be. Fear is the mental chain that binds you, the mental shackles that stop you from going where you want to go and doing what you want to do and being what you want to be. When you allow fear to run your life, you have confined yourself to a self-made prison hole. The fear of not having money can be a slave in itself. Fear is the short lease that stops you from living in the freedom and liberty you have in Christ Jesus. Fear causes us to lose our way. Of all the people in the world, roughly thirty-three percent are Christian. It's fear that stops people from living for God. And sadly, most people in the world have this fear, including too many Christians.

The reason that fear can do these things is because fear is believing. Believing is a law that cannot be broken. You are always believing whether you realize it or not. It is right believing or it is wrong believing. You can change your believing from negative believing (fear) to positive believing. Fear takes you where you don't want to go. Walking in believing, in the light of God's Word, takes you where you do want to go. Fear brings you darkness when you need light. Fear drains and sucks the hope out of any desires, dreams, goals, and ambitions you have. Thus is the power of fear.

When we wake up each day, we ready ourselves for the day. We shower, brush our teeth, style our hair and dress ourselves in the appropriate clothing for whatever job we do, or activity that we have planned. We put on our outer wear. Similarly, we should also clothe our minds with the beauty of the Word of God in order to put off the old man and put on the new man. This is how we rid ourselves of fear or negative believing and change our minds to believe the positive promises of God's Word.

When we conquer our fear and believe God, we not only reap the benefits of God's promises to us, but we also please God by our believing, because without believing it is IMPOSSIBLE to please God. We want to keep the smile of God on our lives. Furthermore, we receive rewards not only in the here and now, but also at the judgment seat (Greek word: *bema*. This word refers to the platform or dias where awards are handed out at the Olympic games.) the place where believers receive their rewards.

Hebrews 11:6

But without faith it is impossible to please him: for he that cometh to God must believe that he is, and that he is a rewarder of them that diligently seek him.

God is a rewarder of those who diligently seek Him. The Greek word for rewarded is misthapodotes. This word means "a giver of wages, a paying in full daily." God wants to give to His kids. God's very nature is to give. He wants to reward us both daily and eternally for our believing. God wants to bless us more than we know – ah, the sunshine of believing.

A renewed mind is a believing mind. Our believing results are directly proportionate to our thinking. Dwelling on darkness will only make the night darker. The body is supposed to be the servant of the mind. A sour face does not just happen; sour face – sour thoughts; happy face – happy thoughts.

There is tremendous power in believing. It's a power we have easy access to. God did not make life so that you have to reach great spiritual heights to believe Him. Many, many common people in God's Word believed for miracles. People who knew very little of God's Word believed. Jesus Christ spent the bulk of his time with and teaching the common man. He himself was a carpenter. Believing is not some mystical, magical principle that is too deep or heavy to do. It is not just for holy men we read about in the Word. It's for all of God's people.

When you're in fellowship with God, you can accomplish anything and overcome everything. God does and will give us the strength to do the things we need to do. That includes the believing to give us the strength to have victory. God is always working with us to give us more hope and to help us grow in our believing and love.

SPIRITUAL GOODIES
For Believing Ye Shall Receive

• Fear ends where believing kicks in.

• You've got to think to get your thinker, thinking. Do you thinketh?

• God is not a respecter of persons. He is a respecter of the conditions you fulfill, like believing and giving.

• Have a few dreams in your heart with God. Christ lived his dream of being Savior of the world. If the desires of your heart are with God they will be the highlights of your life.

• The more you believe, the more you have to be thankful for.

• You can have and do anything you want, you just have to give up the belief that you can't.

• Believing is your receipt and assurance of no failure for you.

• You will never walk with God unless you pray and believe.

• Change your belief and you will change your life.

• You have to believe that believing is the key to receiving or how will you ever believe to receive?

• I can't believe for you, but I can believe with you.

• We become and receive what we believe.

- Confession of belief delivers package of confession.

- God is not partial to unbelief, He is partial to believing.

- Fear erodes and impoverishes believing.

- Believing: you're confident that you could, you trust that you should, you believe that you will, God's word you fulfill.

- Fear: you doubt whether you could, you worry whether you should, you fear that you won't, therefore you don't.

- What excitement it brings when you know you are believing God.

- Your defeats and victories are up to you.

- When you change your thoughts according to God's Word, your whole life will be successfully altered.

- You can go as far and as fast as you want with God. With God, the speed of light is just moseying on you know.

- God's point of view is the only perspective worth looking at.

- There is no better remedy to cure fear than God's love.

- It only took one woman to believe to have the son of God. Mary was the one who rose to the calling.

- You must learn to enjoy life right where you're at. Otherwise, when you get where you're going you will not have learned to enjoy your lot, nor will you have enjoyed the journey.

Chapter Ten
God Heals All Our Diseases

Jesus Christ was tempted with sickness, but was never sick. He was tempted with disease but never contracted a disease. He was tempted to fear, yet lived his life without ever fearing anybody or anything. He was tempted not to love, but all he ever did was love. He never once succumbed to any temptation thrown at him by the devil. Jesus Christ was a perfect savior for all of mankind. The redeemer for whosoever wants eternal life.

1 Peter 2:21 – 24

vs 21   For even hereunto were ye called: because Christ also suffered for us, leaving us an example, that ye should follow his steps:

vs 22   Who did no sin, neither was guile found in his mouth:

vs 23   Who, when he was reviled, reviled not

again; when he suffered, he threatened not; but
committed *himself* to him that judgeth righteously:

vs 24   Who his own self bare our sins in his own
body on the tree, that we, being dead to sins,
should live unto righteousness: by whose stripes ye
were healed.

Because Christ suffered for us, we don't have to. Whether our need is mental, physical, or spiritual, Christ made our deliverance available. There is not one sickness or disease that God does not want us delivered from. This is a promise that needs to be reclaimed in the Christian world. It's our physical well-being and our spiritual birthright. By his stripes you WERE healed. It's already been done; it's already been accomplished for us in Christ Jesus. Christ did not only die for our sins to be forgiven so that we could have eternal life and live with God forever, but he died so that we could also have healthy bodies and sound minds. Let's rise up in our believing, and receive what God has freely given. Don't let that part of what Christ did for YOU be in vain.

God wants us to have a healthy body. And, He desires that we believe Him to obtain this promise. Often when I think of Christ, I see him healing people. And when the people's believing was low, he always helped them rise to the occasion. There has never been anyone better than Christ in helping people grow in their believing to the end that they received deliverance. Multitudes came to Christ often to be delivered of whatever kind of disease they had. No one came to Christ with a sickness or disease, and he said, "Oh that's one I can't heal." There is no new sickness that a person may have from which they can't be delivered. That includes bio-chemical, nuclear, anthrax, you name it – God can heal it. And if Christ tarries, that includes any new ones we don't know about yet.

We don't know the half of all the miracles Christ did. The ones that are recorded in God's word are to help us grow in our believing deliverance. See in your mind's eye Jesus Christ at work. God's heart was always his heart.

Mark 1:21 – 34

vs 21   And they went into Capernaum; and straightway on the sabbath day he entered into the synagogue, and taught.

vs 22   And they were astonished at his doctrine: for he taught them as one that had authority, and not as the scribes.

vs 23   And there was in their synagogue a man with an unclean spirit; and he cried out,

When we spiritually view life, as it really is, like Christ did, we understand life a lot more clearly. Instead, people oftentimes look at life with their five senses; what they can see, hear, smell,

taste, and touch. The spiritual side goes almost totally unde-
tected. When we look at life in light of God's Word, that's when
we will understand it more succinctly and accurately.

> vs 24   Saying, Let us alone; what have we to
> do with thee, thou Jesus of Nazareth? art thou
> come to destroy us? I know thee who thou art,
> the Holy One of God.

> vs 25   And Jesus rebuked him, saying, Hold thy
> peace, and come out of him.

There is a lot more of the spiritual side of life than we know.
It's our spiritual understanding that needs to be enlightened.
Not knowing or understanding what is going on spiritually is
one of the biggest weaknesses in the Christian walk. Reading
what God's people did in the Word, in the spiritual realm, points
out that we have a lot of growing and learning to do. God's Word
gives us instruction on how to walk more like this.

> vs 26   And when the unclean spirit had torn
> him, and cried with a loud voice, he came out
> of him.

> vs 27   And they were all amazed, insomuch
> that they questioned among themselves, saying,
> What thing is this? what new doctrine is this?

> For with authority commandeth he even the
> unclean spirits, and they do obey him.

God would have His people walking like this today. If Christians were to see this today they would say the same thing, "What thing is this? What new doctrine is this?"

> vs 28   And immediately his fame spread abroad
> throughout all the region round about Galilee.

> vs 29   And forthwith, when they were come out
> of the synagogue, they entered into the house of
> Simon and Andrew, with James and John.

> vs 30   But Simon's wife's mother lay sick of a
> fever, and anon they tell him of her.

> vs 31   And he came and took her by the hand,
> and lifted her up; and immediately the fever left
> her, and she ministered unto them.

Unfortunately, sometimes touch can feel very creepy and disturbing. Most of us have had an experience when someone touched us and something just wasn't right. However, when you're walking in love there can be a lot of healing in touch. In this situation, touch was part of what caused this miracle. The power of touch when it is the love of God can be astoundingly full of healing power.

One moment Peter's mother-in-law is laying there sick of a fever and the next moment she is totally healed and is up and ministering to THEM! It's available to have a fever and have it leave just that quickly. You can't minister and bless much when you are lying flat on your back. When you are sick to the point that you just don't feel like doing anything, you cannot help yourself or anyone else. When the fever left she ministered and gave.

> vs 32   And at even, when the sun did set, they brought unto him all that were diseased, and them that were possessed with devils.

> vs 33   And all the city was gathered together at the door.

> vs 34   And he healed many that were sick of divers diseases, and cast out many devils; and suffered not the devils to speak, because they knew him.

When Jesus Christ walked on the earth, he taught a new way to love and give and serve God. He spent a great deal of time healing people during his public ministry. He set the standard for God's heart toward people. There is no question about it, God desires for his people to be healthy and healed in mind and body. Spiritually, things need a lot more cleaning up than we know.

The apostles learned all about healing from Jesus Christ. They understood what was required to receive the promises from God. Look at what they asked Jesus Christ for. We should all be asking for the same.

Luke 17:5, 12 – 19

vs 5   And the apostles said unto the Lord, Increase our faith.

Increasing our faith (believing) is something we all need more of. Lack of it is why we don't get answers to prayer. When we don't have believing, the very things we want to happen don't. The apostles were saying to Jesus Christ, "We need to increase our believing so we can help and do the miracles and wonders you do." These men wanted to be more like Christ. That's why these men were chosen by God to follow Christ. It's in believing that we get things done, that our prayers are answered. The disciples knew Christ's power came from believing God. They wanted to live like he did and fellowship with God the way he did.

vs 12   And as he entered into a certain village, there met him ten men that were lepers, which stood afar off:

vs 13   And they lifted up their voices, and said, Jesus, Master, have mercy on us.

vs 14   And when he saw them, he said unto
them, Go shew yourselves unto the priests.
And it came to pass, that, as they went, they
were cleansed.

They did not get healed instantaneously. They ACTED first
on what Christ said and then got their healing as they went.

vs 15   And one of them, when he saw that he
was healed, turned back, and with a loud voice
glorified God,

vs 16   And fell down on his face at his feet, giving him thanks: and he was a Samaritan.

Only one of the healed lepers came back to give glory to
God. He was thankful and he acknowledged it, regardless of
what anyone else thought. The humbleness and thankfulness in
the soul of this man caused him to bow down and give thanks
to Christ.

vs 17   And Jesus answering said, Were there
not ten cleansed? but where are the nine?

vs 18   There are not found that returned to give
glory to God, save this stranger.

vs 19   And he said unto him, Arise, go thy way:
thy faith hath made thee whole

They were all healed but only one was made whole. The word "whole" in the Greek is *sozo*: it means, every part made whole. He received a miracle of the healing of the mind which the others did not. He was made whole mentally as well as physically. He received by far the greatest blessing. This would have helped this man for the rest of his life.

Let's look at another amazing record of Jesus Christ healing someone.

Luke 7:1 – 10

vs 1   Now when he had ended all his sayings in the audience of the people, he entered into Capernaum.

vs 2   And a certain centurion's servant, who was dear unto him, was sick, and ready to die.

vs 3   And when he heard of Jesus, he sent unto him the elders of the Jews, beseeching him that he would come and heal his servant.

vs 4   And when they came to Jesus, they besought him instantly, saying, That he was worthy for whom he should do this:

vs 5   For he loveth our nation, and he hath built us a synagogue.

vs 6   Then Jesus went with them. And when
he was now not far from the house, the centurion sent friends to him, saying unto him, Lord,
trouble not thyself: for I am not worthy that
thou shouldest enter under my roof:

vs 7   Wherefore neither thought I myself
worthy [to regard as deserving, hold worthy of]
to come unto thee: but say in a word, and my
servant shall be healed.

The believing that this man had is amazing! You know, it is
love that energizes our believing. He had great love for his servant, believed for him to be healed and yet he felt unworthy. It
seems like most of us don't consider ourselves worthy either. The
difference between him and us seems to be that he loved enough
to believe. Let us love believe and realize that we are worthy.
Through the eyes of love, believing is brought into fruition.

vs 8   For I also am a man set under authority,
having under me soldiers, and I say unto one,
Go, and he goeth; and to another, Come, and
he cometh; and to my servant, Do this, and he
doeth it.

This centurion understood authority. Authority comes from
the law. He knew that when he commanded someone under

him in authority that they had to do as he said. It was the law. He transferred this understanding of authority to believing. He understood that believing was a law.

> vs 9   When Jesus heard these things, he mar-
> velled at him, and turned him about, and said
> unto the people that followed him, I say unto you,
> I have not found so great faith, no, not in Israel.

This is the kind of believing we should desire to have, the kind that Christ marveled at.

> vs 10   And they that were sent, returning to the
> house, found the servant whole that had been sick.

I bet these friends of the centurion were doing double time back to the house to see the servant after what Christ said! I would have loved to have spent the rest of the day at that house. Imagine the thankfulness and the jubilation! It's believing that pleases God and brings the desired results.

Psalm 103:3

> Who forgiveth all thine iniquities; who healeth
> all thy diseases.

It is God, Who forgives and heals. That is the love and heart of God toward you and me. He forgiveth ALL our iniquities without exception. God healeth ALL thy diseases without exception. Christians believe they are forgiven by the blood Christ spilled, but have been talked out of their health and healing which was given to them by the beating and stripes Christ bore for us. One promise is as true as the other. Health is as available as forgiveness. God's people have been cheated out of their health by the devil for way too long. Let's claim our health according to God's Word.

SPIRITUAL GOODIES
For God Heals All Our Diseases

- When you talk to God and you want Him to reciprocate. His only condition is that you believe. God is looking for fellowship and conversation, that's why He made us.

- How you feel has everything to do with how you think. God gave us feelings and emotions, they can be a good thing if you want them to be.

- God put us on this earth to succeed not fail.

- Bitterness is like a cavity, if it is not taken care of it will affect the whole body.

- If you never did another thing for God or His people for the rest of your life, God will not love you any less than if you served Him for the rest of your life. That's God's standard of what love is.

- The best ingredients and remedy for healing your wound are forgiveness and forgetfulness.

- The world has cheated God's people for too long.

- You won't change your life until you change your thinking.

- When you're believing God and He opens doors for you, don't allow the adversary to slip in and cause you to become doubtful lest your believing slips through your fingers.

- God's love is all He says it is.

- God is personal and always present. We are never absent in God's thoughts or heart.

- God made us with ears so we would here His Word and eyes so we could see His love.

- God's understanding is infinite, measureless, without limits or bounds. His understanding is endless and fathomless. Hang out with Someone who really knows it all.

- By far, God's Word has more power to deliver you of your worries and fears than anything else.

- The Bible is the best health book you will ever read.

- I've worked so hard for so long to arrive at a healthy body, I fear now I have a flabby mind.

- You can't have the love of God without the truth of God.

- Every time we say something about the Word of God that is not the truth, we are telling lies about God. Does it matter? It matters to God!

Chapter Eleven

God First

Jesus Christ was the role model for putting God first. He was the only man who ever walked the face of the earth who always put God first. He lived putting God first flawlessly. He never wanted for anything and his fellowship with God was the sweetest this side of heaven. So when he taught about putting God first, he spoke the greatest truth ever told to man about how to live God first. He captured the heart of love in service to God and he shared it with his disciples in Matthew six. Putting God first in our lives will make our fellowship with God sweet and our peace of mind complete. It will cause us to have all our needs met without fear and anxiety. This section of Matthew exemplifies one of God's truly magnificent promises.

Matthew 6:24 – 34

vs 24   No man can serve two masters: for either he will hate the one, and love the other;

or else he will hold to the one, and despise the
other. Ye cannot serve God and mammon.

The man in this verse is an all-inclusive noun, no one can.
God is one master, mammon the other master. Mammon in the
Greek is *mammonas*. It is wealth and riches. It represents all the
material things of the world. You can't live for the world and
serve God. One master WILL prevail. It's your decision which
one it is. No one is able to do both. If you sell out to the world,
you won't like God and you will grow to despise Him. Or you
can choose to love and serve God and live life to the fullest.

When you look words up in the Greek and the Hebrew, it's
an indispensable resource in learning God's Word. It is vital to
our understanding to learn the whys and wherefores of different words that are used in God's Word. You see a lot more of
God's heart in the utilization of looking up individual words.
Just make sure that you use good Greek and Hebrew reference
books. Just look at how much more insight the following Greek
words give us.

The word "serve" is used twice in this verse. It is the Greek
word *douleuo*: it means slave, bondage, do service, slavery. This
word has an upside and a down side to it. It's like the word love;
you just have to be careful what you love. God does not want us
to be slaves to the world. When you are enslaved to the world,
it is bondage and slavery to your life. In serving mammon you

become a slave to sin. The world will fill you with anxiety and misery. You will never have happiness or be fulfilled.

I once worked for a man who was a Christian. He spent all most all his time working like a slave for the material realm. He lived in a great home, in a great neighborhood. One night about 2:00 a.m. he was working at his desk and he had a heart attack. He thought he was going to die. It changed his perspective on life. He told me, "I now work forty hours a week and less if I can. Now I spend time with my family and attend church." His goal had been to make a million bucks that year. One master was prevailing and almost prevailed.

Also, part of the meaning of this word "serve" includes actions which are directed by others. And, in this man's case, it was not the good master directing his actions. God always looks on the heart. There is nothing wrong with wanting to make a million dollars. If you made fifty thousand a year for the next twenty years you made a million. If you made a hundred thousand a year – and so on, you do the math. You could make a million dollars overnight, if your heart is right (not perfect) toward God. God just wants to help us in our lives while we're here. He just wants us to keep Him first. We are the ones who will benefit from living God first. You will love and serve something. Verse twenty-four contains the depth of the first and great commandment.

Mark 12:30

And thou shalt love the Lord thy God with all thy heart, and with all thy soul, and with all thy mind, and with all thy strength: this *is* the first commandment.

God wants us to love Him and hold on to Him. He wants us to seek His kingdom first. The greatest freedom and living of life there is, is in giving service to God. Most of our serving God is in the daily "highways and byways" of life not in church or the class room.

Matthew 6:25 - 31

vs 25   Therefore I say unto you, Take no thought for your life, what ye shall eat, or what ye shall drink; nor yet for your body, what ye shall put on. Is not the life more than meat, and the body than raiment?

The Greek word for thought is *merimnao*. It means to be full of anxiety, which divides up and distracts the mind, anxious thoughts, to be troubled with cares. These cares distract the heart and mind. This same word is used six times in this chapter. God wants to free us from this kind of thinking. Don't have anxiety filled thoughts about your food and drink or the clothes you wear. Don't be all consumed, or over anxious with what you are going to eat and wear. God is showing us how we can live without anxiety in these areas of our lives.

> vs 26   Behold the fowls of the air: for they sow
> not, neither do they reap, nor gather into barns;
> yet your heavenly Father feedeth them. Are ye
> not much better than they?

God is wearing his heart on His sleeve in this verse. God feeds the birds of the air. He set the order of life up so the birds would have enough to eat. Are we not much better than the birds? We're a lot different to God than birds. When you see birds it will bless you to think about this verse.

God helped Jesus Christ reach the hearts of the people all the time. God told him what words to speak. He often used many natural settings around him to teach his disciples. The word "behold" is calling our attention to the importance of a specific truth. When I read the words that Christ spoke, "Behold the fowls of the air . . . ," all I can see is a flock of birds flying around, good healthy looking birds. Look at the birds around you. They don't look like they are having any anxious thoughts. Just for fun I stepped outside to see all the anxiety filled birds. They were all singing like they didn't have a care in the world. I felt like they were looking at me thinking, "Don't you wish you could fly?". They are not worried about what food they will eat or what they're going to wear, I promise you that. None of the birds I see look homeless. None of them look like they just came from the soup line or unemployment line. They all look so happy – like they don't have a bill in the world or ever will have. They seem to land where they like and just start eating, and God knows what. I looked high and low didn't find one worried bird.

> vs 27   Which of you by taking thought [anx-
> ious or anxiety filled thought] can add one cubit
> unto his stature?

No matter how anxious you are or how much you worry, it will not help you one bit in having the things you need in life. Keep the verse in its context; the law of reverse effort will set in if you spend too much anxiety thought time on those needs. The very thing you want to happen won't. In fact, the exact opposite of what you are trying to get, can happen. An anxious thought will add nothing to your height, or aid one bit in your prosper-ing. So why be like that when it's available to live without it.

> vs 28   And why take ye thought [anxious, ner-
> vous thought] for raiment? Consider the lilies
> of the field, how they grow; [growth without
> compulsion] they toil not, neither do they spin:

A flower doesn't say to itself, "Okay now, push those shoots up. Grow those leaves." It just blossoms into a beautiful flower that God made.

> vs 29   And yet I say unto you, That even
> Solomon in all his glory was not arrayed like
> one of these.

Jesus Christ is pointing out the beauty of the flower that just grows. Even with all that Solomon had, and no man on this earth will ever have the wealth Solomon had, the flowers are more magnificent. I think it's wonderful that Solomon, who was one of God's people, had more than anyone else ever had or will have in this life.

> vs 30   Wherefore, if God so clothe the grass of
> the field, which to day is, and to morrow is cast
> into the oven, shall he not much more clothe
> you, O ye of little faith?

I don't know about you, but I don't want God referring to me as little believer.

> vs 31   Therefore take no thought, [anxious
> thought] saying, What shall we eat? or, What shall
> we drink? or, Wherewithal shall we be clothed?

It's supposed to be a blessing when you think about your clothing. We can be thankful when we ask what's to eat, because we're talking about variety. Many of the people in the world struggle with getting something to eat, and having enough food to stay alive. If you will take God at His Word and trust Him, you will not starve to death. You will also have good water to drink. America has an abundance of food. God has blessed this land and it produces some of the finest food in the world in quality and quantity – personally I think the best. Food is to be enjoyed by the hand of God, as also the garb we wear and the beverages we drink.

Ecclesiastes 5:18 & 19

Behold that which I have seen: it is good and comely for one to eat and to drink, and to enjoy the good of all his labour that he taketh under the sun all the days of his life, which God giveth him: for it is his portion.

Every man also to whom God hath given riches and wealth, and hath given him power to eat thereof, and to take his portion, and to rejoice in his labour; this is the gift of God.

What amazing promises God has made to us in His Word. It is our portion. God will bless us with food and drink and we can rejoice in our labor. He wants to give to His people riches and wealth. So why be anxious?

The Word says to have some wine for your stomach's sake. Maybe your stomach is really hurting today because of your anxiety thoughts, so you need little extra. And you women don't have anxiety over which one of the fifty outfits you're going to wear.

Matthew 6:32 - 34

vs 32   (For after all these things do the Gentiles
seek:) for your heavenly Father knoweth that
ye have need of all these things.

The Gentiles are the unbelievers of the world. In this section of God's Word God is showing us how the unsaved live, and
we are not to live like them. This is how the God rejecter lives;
they are slaves to the material realm. You can see that's all the
unsaved seek. It's slavery and bondage to the world. It's people
with greediness and living selfishly. I like the words piggishness
and hoggishness. It's the natural man's ignorance and dilemma.
Without God this is man's natural state. And it's only the Word
of God that will change it.

Jesus Christ spent time teaching his disciples this, to bring
them to this pinnacle promise. This is the how, the way to live
life so God can take care of us, His kids, as a Father wants to do
for His children.

vs 33   But [in contrast to everything Christ
just said] seek ye first the kingdom of God, and
his righteousness; and all these things shall be
added unto you.

If you seek anything else first, you will live like the Gentiles. And as a result, the law of reverse effort sets in. The harder

you try with anxiety filled thoughts the less you have, and the more miserable you become. God said if you seek Him first, all of these things will be added unto you. The cry of God to His people is, "Trust your heavenly Father!" We don't have to be a slave to the company store. Putting God first is the key to enjoying the things God has blessed us with. Putting God first does more for a person's happiness, joyfulness and the peace in your soul and mind, than anything else in life. Putting God first is the biggest, fastest believing builder I know. Elevating God to this position stops more problems and solves more problems than we can perceive.

> vs 34   Take therefore no thought [anxious
> thought] for the morrow: for the morrow shall
> take thought [anxious thought] for the things of
> itself. Sufficient unto the day is the evil thereof.

What love and healing wisdom this verse gives. Live one day at a time. None of us can change yesterday, turn back the hands of time or start living tomorrow, today. "Sufficient unto the day is the evil thereof." There is enough trouble today to deal with. Sufficient for each day is its own trouble. God with all His understanding is teaching us how to best live life. How we can live life to the fullest, and live the more abundant life Jesus Christ made available one day at a time.

Having some love and respect for God will get us on the

right track of putting Him first in our lives. God FIRST before anyone or anything! God precedes all others in time, order and/ or importance. As you get older what thoughts could comfort and bless you more than knowing you had endeavored to put God first in your life. When you look at your life in the "rearview mirror" will you see that God was first in your life? Don't let hindsight be the clearest, it doesn't have to be.

SPIRITUAL GOODIES For God First

- Time spent with God in His word is time well spent, it's never wasted.

- There is no understanding that will bless a man more than spiritual understanding which only comes from God and His Word.

- Money can be an awesome servant or an evil master.

- You cannot purchase or buy ONE heavenly treasure.

- The greatest thing you will ever be a member of is the family of God. It says in Corinthians we are members in particular. It seems like being a member of anything else is bondage. What's most important in the body of Christ is your function, not your title or position. There will be a lot of wonderful hearted Christians that receive more rewards at Christ's return than many of those with big titles. Always remember God looks on the heart.

- Make sure your walking in love when you say in your heart, "I will have no friends when it comes to the truth of God's Word." Remember its love that covers a multitude of sins, and the only people there are, are "multitude" people. That's what God said and I am going to roll with Him.

- The sweetest memories you will ever have are the things you did with God and for God.

- There are no denominations in God's eyes. Denominations are man-made. It's one family under God, the family of God. Christianity is what God wrought in Christ Jesus.

I Corinthians 1:12

Now this I say, that every one of you saith, I am of Paul; and I of Apollos; and I of Cephas [Peter] and I of Christ.

- The people were causing the divisions, but Paul endeavored to hold the line. Looks like the first denominations to me. We are one family before God. And when we get to heaven that will not change.

- Unconditional love cannot be understood outside of the love of God.

- Remember to thank God often, it goes further than we know. A thankful heart goes a long way with God. It's like love covers a multitude of sins.

- I wonder how much thanking we would do if we could see all the times God stopped the devil from doing what he would have done.

- Religion puts you in bondage, and it's one of the cruelest things in life.

- Don't confuse religion with spirituality. Spirituality is our relationship with God.

- When God blesses you with something, it's always His heart behind it that blesses you most of all.

- You will never get any closer to the heart of God than His Word.

- God is going to be the only object of my worship.

- The excitement in obedience to God is waiting to see what He had in mind.

- Thank God for His light to shine upon your path so you will know where to go and what to do. The glory of the Lord did LIGHTEN the path.

Isaiah 60:19

The sun shall be no more thy light by day;
neither for brightness shall the moon give light
unto thee: but the LORD shall be unto thee an
everlasting light, and thy God thy glory.

Isaiah 60:20

Thy sun shall no more go down; neither shall thy moon withdraw itself: for the LORD shall be thine everlasting light, and the days of thy mourning shall be ended.

Rev. 22:5

And there shall be no night there; and they need no candle, neither light of the sun; for the Lord God giveth them light: and they shall reign for ever and ever.

- Man is spiritually blind without God's light. Without spiritual light you will walk in spiritual darkness.

- Light can be measured. How can darkness be measured?

- God has an economic blueprint that will work for everyone.

- Only God has the answer to the meaning of life. He's the only one that can make life meaningful.

- Where have you placed God in your heart? How important and what value do you put on that relationship? If He's not first, you have another god before Him.

- Learn to enjoy the little things in life, and then when God brings the big things you will have joy unspeakable.

- We will always gravitate toward that which we love.

- God wants us to love Him with the same love He loves us with, the spiritual love He gave us. Love Him with the Christ in you by way of the renewed mind.

Mark 12:30

And thou shalt love the Lord thy God with all thy heart, and with all thy soul, and with all thy mind, and with all thy strength: this is the first commandment.

- God also loves us with all His heart, and with all His Being, and with all His thinking, and with all His strength.

- Those who walk in the love of God will receive the greatest eternal rewards in heaven.

- From time to time, there is one thing about this life that sorrows me. No matter where you go, what groups you associate with, you can't get away from the religion of sin. Even if you started to set your ministry up to the perfection and standard of the Word on how it is to function, religion would be there before you saw it. It's man's sin nature. Until Christ comes back we will always have rules, regulations, policies, procedures, and laws in the church which no one can follow or keep perfectly. Thank God the only thing I am a member of is the body of Christ. You could throw me out of your church or out of your group or disassociate yourself with me. Hoopa. No one can be thrown out of the body of Christ. And to man God says, "How you like them apples? That's for all my kids!" Well, that's not a quote, but that's the gist of it. It's sad that we all fall prey to the religion of rules and regulations. It's what brings about distrust, jealousy, strife, and our greatest sin, the lack of love one for another. No matter what group or organization, man's weaknesses and frailties are evident. When was the last time that you remember a person loving you with God's love in all it's purity with no ulterior motive? Can you think of a time when you walked away thinking, "I don't ever recall being loved like that before." What stops us from loving like that is the old man nature we are always dragging around with us. All the creeds of religion will be here no matter where you go until Christ comes back. In Ephesians 5:1 and 2, God says, "Be ye therefore followers of God, as dear children; and walk in love . . ." God is not requesting for us to walk in love in this verse, it is a command. We are to be follows of God, not a ministry, denomination, church, group or man. There is as much difference following God and following man as there is between night and day. One is religion, the other is what God wrought in Christ Jesus our Lord. Even though this is true, God wants us to dwell on the positives of His Word.

Philippians 4:8

Finally, brethren, whatsoever things are true, whatsoever things are honest, whatsoever things are just, whatsoever things are pure, whatsoever things are lovely, whatsoever things are of good report; if there be any virtue, and if there be any praise, think on these things.

- If we showed our minister half the love we give our dog or cat, things would be a lot better. Let's all remember God sent just one perfect minister who taught and helped God's people. Jesus Christ was our substitute for death so we could live a more abundant life. We have to fight the devil together because that's where all the evil comes from. The number three in the Word means complete and the devil's outreach is complete. He steals, kills and destroys. We are all in this together as one family.

Romans 7:14 - 18

vs 14   For we know that the law is spiritual: but I am carnal, sold under sin.

vs 15   For that which I do I allow not: for what
I would, that do I not; but what I hate, that do I.

vs 16   If then I do that which I would not, I
consent unto the law that it is good.

vs 17   Now then it is no more I that do it, but
sin that dwelleth in me.

vs 18   For I know that in me (that is, in my
flesh,) dwelleth no good thing: for to will is
present with me; but how to perform that which
is good I find not.

• This part of life will only change with the return of Christ.
Thank God we have the hope of eternal life. We can be
thankful for every day.

Chapter Twelve
Healing is Always a Gift

God wants us to believe for healing, like all of the rest of the people who have received healing. We just need to grow in our believing to receive. God is always willing to help us in our believing images of victory. We need to believingly picture ourselves completely healthy. God's compassion for our well being has not changed. The people we read about in God's Word wanted deliverance. God's will for us is deliverance as well.

Matthew 12:9 – 13

vs 9   And when he was departed thence, he went into their synagogue:

vs 10   And, behold, there was a man which had his hand withered. And they asked him, saying, Is it lawful to heal on the sabbath days? that they might accuse him.

Why do the accusers always seem to be around watching you to see if you do something wrong, or accuse you for the right you are doing?

> vs 11   And he said unto them, What man shall there be among you, that shall have one sheep, and if it fall into a pit on the sabbath day, will he not lay hold on it, and lift it out?

> vs 12   How much then is a man better than a sheep? Wherefore it is lawful to do well on the sabbath days.

Whenever you're doing something good for God, embittered and heartless people will usually be around. God is always fighting for us and the devil is always fighting against us.

> vs 13   Then saith he to the man, Stretch forth thine hand. And he stretched it forth; and it was restored whole, like as the other.

How blessed would you be, if you were in his shoes? As we read records in God's Word on healing, it builds believing. These people had heard of other people being healed, and the stories of their deliverance helped build their trust to the point of believing to receive deliverance. They knew others who had sicknesses and impairments and then saw them completely set free, totally delivered. The man in this record had heard enough to overcome his unbelief. Most of these people are just common everyday people, just like us.

Romans 10:17

So then faith cometh by hearing, and hearing by the word of God.

We have to hear enough of the truth of God's Word in order to believe. How much we need to hear is going to vary from one person to another. Only you can determine that. No one else can do that for you. Do we want deliverance, or have we just become content to live with our sickness and disease? Have we given up on the truth from God that deliverance is readily available? Don't quit, with God all things are possible. And it's your believing that pleases God.

Acts 10:38

How God anointed Jesus of Nazareth with the Holy Ghost and with power: who went about doing good, and healing all that were oppressed of the devil; for God was with him.

Jesus Christ set the example of how to help God's people. He went around healing all that were oppressed of the devil. God's Word points the finger at where sickness comes from. Remember it's the devil that oppresses and wants to overpower us in the category of our health. Therefore, we can see in God's Word that God always wants His people to be healed. That's why God sent Christ.

Matthew 12:22

Then was brought unto him one possessed with a devil, blind, and dumb: and he healed him, insomuch that the blind and dumb both spake and saw.

I'm so glad to see a verse like this because now I know there's still hope for me. To be blind and then be able to physically see, how thankful would you be? Imagine what it would be like to not be able to speak and then to be healed and be able to talk. Think of all the wonderful things you could tell people. There would be so many things you always wanted to say, but couldn't. Maybe some people were not so nice to you and they might get an earful. Imagine the joy of being able to literally speak the Word of God for the first time, to hear it from your own lips with your voice telling of God's healing deliverance.

When God healed these people they did not have to work on the pronunciation of their words either. These people would have spoken as plainly and clearly as anybody else. Vocal cords or whatever it was that needed healing was healed by the power of God by a miracle. These people would have had beautiful and unique voices that people would have loved to hear. When God performs miracles it's never mundane or bland.

Psalm 67:2

That thy way may be known [learn to know,
find out] upon earth, [whole earth as opposed
to a part] thy saving [deliverance, help] health
among all nations.

God's way is His saving health to His people. And, He wants
it to be known amongst all the people of the earth. It's the way
God is. God wants and desires for us and our children to have
good health much more than we want it for ourselves. Our
health is to be enjoyed, compliments of God.

Psalm 103:3

Who forgiveth all thine iniquities; who healeth
all thy diseases;

God forgives ALL of your sins, even the same ones you continue to make over and over again. There are a lot of diseases
today that medicine does not heal. God heals all, free of charge.
And, the medicines that do cure, well, they are made from the
resources that God put in the earth. Let's give credit where it is
do. It is just another way of God showing His love for all people.
All the antibiotics and medicines that man makes, all of them,
come out of the earth that God made.

We often hear the word "create" today. People say that inven-
tors "create" products, artists "create" masterpieces, research-

ers "create" new drugs, etc. Man does not "create" anything. In Genesis God defines "create" as making something from nothing. Man always starts with something. When God creates He starts with absolutely nothing. Man cannot do that. Man uses this word haphazardly and surreptitiously. Let's use this word "create" correctly. Only God can create. We take what God has already created and use it as a resource to develop something.

Ezekiel 47:12

And by the river upon the bank thereof, on this
side and on that side, shall grow all trees for
meat, whose leaf shall not fade, neither shall the
fruit thereof be consumed: it shall bring forth
new fruit according to his months, because their
waters they issued out of the sanctuary: and
the fruit thereof shall be for meat, and the leaf
thereof for medicine.

If I knew what tree this was I would be having a leaf lunch, with no dressing. I would not care what it tastes like. There is a lot more healing in the things God made in their natural state than we know. We need to continue to believe God and find them. There are combinations of things only God knows that will heal people.

A good example is the discovery of penicillin. Penicillin was discovered accidentally in 1928 by Sir Alexander Fleming when he was conducting experiments in his laboratory in petri dishes. He noticed that microbes in some of his cultures were killed off by the growth of Penicillin mold. He was able to extract the effective substances and "penicillin" became the first dedicated antibiotic drug. A lot of grandparents are here today because of penicillin. I know Someone who would say it didn't happen accidentally.

Psalm 107:20

He sent his word, and healed them, and delivered them from their destructions.

If people are going to get healed, it's going to be because of the word that God sent. It's the Word of God that builds a person's believing to be able to overcome. You first have to believe that healing is available. You have to believe that it truly is God's will. The best way I know to help people in their lives where they need help is to help them fill their mind with the positives from God's Word in that area. And, in order to fill our minds with God's Word, we need to have it in front of our eyes. Make copies of verses on healing, and carry them with you. Put them on your fridge so that you can fill your mind with God's Word while you're looking for something to satisfy your appetite. Put verses on your mirror – not your rear view mirror, lol. Carry fifty verses with you and memorize some of them. Fill your mind with the health and healing that comes from God. Listen to CDs on health and healing. Make sure that they are quality teachings that build your believing. My endeavor is to help you live the more abundant life, in any area I can. Believing increases believing.

The previous verse says, " . . . delivered them from their destructions." It doesn't say IF they get into destructions, God will deliver them. Nope, we get into them because it is the natural state of man. It is our sin nature. We needed deliverance from our own destructions and we continue to need it.

The only reason anybody ever gets healed is because God loves us. Whenever anyone gets healed, it is always a gift. Even when animals get healed it's a gift from God. Why? It is because God made the body to heal itself. If he hadn't, a small nick on your finger would cause you to bleed to death. What love our Father has for us.

Proverbs 17:22

A merry heart doeth good like a medicine: [a cure, a healing, removal of bondage] but a broken spirit drieth the bones.

Our believing attitude does more for our health than we know. The words, "merry heart" means in the inner most part of your soul you are happy and rejoicing. What are you happy and rejoicing about? You rejoice about God's Word and all that He has done for you. To live believing that you are blessed by God is very healing to the physical body. It's like a medicine to our bones where the blood is manufactured.

After the word medicine is the word "but." The word "but" sets in contrast that which is written before to that which is coming next. It sets a contrast between "a merry heart" and "a broken spirit." Have you ever seen a man or woman who is broken? It's as if you can see the weight lying upon them. They give off defeat and agony. All hope is gone. What a contrast to a merry heart.

A broken spirit dries the bones. The human body is 60 to 70 percent water and our bones are 10 to 15 percent water. Our blood cells are manufactured in the bones. Dry or brittle bones break easier and the blood that is manufactured in them is not the quality of blood that is made with bones that have the right amount of water. These bones do not manufacture the white blood cells appropriate for fighting off disease.

When we have a merry heart toward God and His Word we have health, but when we are defeated by the negatives of the world and we are broken down, our health is endangered. If you want a healthy body, get the healthiest thoughts you can get. Only the best thoughts come from God's Word.

The greatest blessing in this life, is the conviction in your soul that you are loved by God Himself. It's the Word of God living in people's lives that produces results. Everything else produces nothing. You cannot separate God's Word and God Himself. You cannot separate God from His Word. You can get no closer to God than His Word. It's how we know Him and fellowship with Him.

We are all moving on down the road in years – time marches

on. Let's not look back and be more disappointed by the things we didn't do than by the things we did. Don't wait until it is too late and you have lilies on your brow.

Psalm 118:24

This is the day which the LORD hath made; we
will rejoice and be glad in it.

Today is a day God made for you, will you rejoice and be glad in it? The people this verse is written about declared, "WE WILL." That's the kind of company I want to keep. There is so much healing in living this way.

SPIRITUAL GOODIES
For Healing is Always a Gift

- The greatest things that are done in life are for God and His people.

- Love is the switch that inactivates fear.

- Mothers do more forgiving than anyone else.

- Get your eyes off your own inadequacies and onto God.

- You cannot lay a believing egg by straining.

- The best friends I have are those who bring me closer to the heart of God.

- Do things for people often with no strings attached or any ulterior motives. You will enjoy life more.

- The cultivation of a merry heart is health to the soul.

- The love of God never fails. The only failure you could have with this verse is the failure of endeavoring to live it.

- Love is something you can give away and you end up with more of.

- God's Word is God's written Will for our lives now.

- We all want our lives to account for something. And so does God.

Chapter Thirteen

Forgiveness by Grace

Everyone needs to know on a daily basis that we are forgiven. The fear that comes from thinking we are unforgivable by God is more than a person should bear. How could you live with the thought of being lost forever? The pressure and the pain that is lifted from our hearts, is so freeing when we know that we are forgiven. It is very healing to know that God Himself has forgiven us of every sin we have ever committed and every sin that we are going to commit. We have not committed one sin that we are not forgiven for. It's that forgiveness from God that frees us from guilt, shame and the thought of being lost. To know that God does not condemn or judge us daily, is delivering. The wondrous taste and sweetness of forgiveness, is a burden relinquished. God has made us all forgivable in His sight. His perfect son, our brother Jesus Christ, accomplished that for us.

God calls Himself many things in His word: God is Spirit, God is Love, God is Light and the greatest thing God is, is Holy Spirit. If we do love God, it is because He loved us first. God does not treat us as guilty, nor is He incriminating toward us. It is never God's will that we carry a feeling of self-reproach. To wonder if we are forgiven brings little or no relief to our hearts. It's the conviction in our souls that we are completely pardoned for every evil thought and act that brings rest and comfort to the soul.

Ephesians 1:7

In whom we have redemption through his
blood, the forgiveness of sins, according to the
riches of his grace;

Our Father's open heartedness to lovingly forgive us brings great joy to the heart and life of a man or women. God has no resentment toward us nor does He desire to punish us. God rescued us when we needed rescuing. When we need forgiveness, God is always first in line to forgive. Too often the rest of us are somewhere down the line. Some never get in line. We should be second in that line to forgive our own selves. Sometimes it's only the person and God that knows what they thought or did. If we can't learn to forgive ourselves we're going to have a really hard time pardoning others. What we don't like in ourselves, we seem to hate in others. Our worst crimes are the hardest things to say we're sorry for.

There is so much mental exhaustion and drain in not forgiving others day after day. When we don't forgive, we continue to suffer as the victim. We don't hold onto the bitterness, it holds onto us. When we don't move from bitterness, it fuels anger which can lead to actions that are potentially costly. Only God can cleanse the stain of bitterness.

If we never sinned, what would we have to be forgiven for? God knew full well none of us would be able to live like that. We all know someone who never had to forgive himself. That would be our eldest brother, Jesus Christ. All he ever did was love. That's why we were given the Savior of forgiveness, the captain of our salvation, our forgiving brother, Jesus Christ.

Sometimes in life it may seem like just God and His wonderful son are the only ones who have forgiven you. God's Word teaches what forgiveness really is. Let's take a look at this wonderful record of forgiveness.

John 8:1 – 11

vs 1   Jesus went unto the mount of Olives.

vs 2   And early in the morning he came again into the temple, and all the people came unto him; and he sat down, and taught them.

vs 3   And the scribes and Pharisees brought unto him a women taken in adultery; and when they had set her in the midst,

vs 4   They say unto him, Master, this women was taken in adultery, in the very act.

I wonder why they let the man or men go and just brought the woman? Surely none of her accusers were part of the act.

> vs 5   Now Moses in the law commanded us,
> that such should be stoned: but what sayest thou?

> vs 6   This they said, tempting him, that they
> might have to accuse him. But Jesus stooped
> down, and with *his* finger wrote on the ground,
> *as though he heard them not.*

> vs 7   So when they continued asking him, he
> lifted up himself, and said unto them, He that is
> without sin among you, let him first cast a stone
> at her.

> vs 8   And again he stooped down, and wrote
> on the ground.

> vs 9   And they which heard *it,* being convicted
> by *their own* conscience, went out one by one,
> beginning at the eldest, *even* unto the last: and
> Jesus was left alone, and the women standing in
> the midst.

The oldest left first. Usually with age comes a little more wisdom. Older people are also generally more afraid of death which seems to be the topic of discussion in this record.

vs 10   When Jesus had lifted up himself, and saw none but the woman, he said unto her, Woman, where are those thine accusers? hath no man condemned thee?

vs 11   She said, No man, Lord. And Jesus said unto her, Neither do I condemn thee: go, and sin no more.

The lifesaving words that Christ spoke to her in her hour of need, in this life or death situation were, "Neither do I condemn thee." What those words must have meant to this woman on that day. He was her savior, her redeemer. He caused all her accusers to depart. She got a taste of the love and forgiveness of God on that glorious day. Wherever the savior is, there is forgiveness and life available.

He treated her as though she was not guilty. Christ forgave her. It was she and Christ. No one manifested more forgiveness than Christ. She would have heard it in the tone of his voice, saw it in his eyes and facial expression, and seen it in his demeanor. Jesus Christ had great willingness to forgive and bless her. The love of God sees more, but is willing to see less. We talk about the bad things people say about us. When is the last time you were in the midst of a crowd and they all wanted to stone you to death? I've been shot at, and I would take that any day over this situation, unless Christ was there.

We all need forgiveness more than we would like to admit. Forgiveness makes a man stronger, and liked more. Jesus Christ was the biggest believer in forgiving sin. The greatest act of love to man from God is His forgiveness. And, the greatest gift He ever gave man is to live with Him forever; the gift of eternal life. Where God lives, there will be no condemning nor will there be the need for forgiveness. The best time you have ever had on earth and/or the highlight of your life will pale in comparison to eternity in Heaven.

Ephesians 4: 32

And be ye kind one to another, tenderhearted,
forgiving one another, even as God for Christ's
sake hath forgiven you.

The reason we find it hard to forgive others, is because we have forgotten what God has forgiven us for. Forgiving one another is a language the deaf can hear and the blind can see. Forgiveness does not change the past, it brightens the present and illuminates the future. To be pardoned is often needed in the life and soul of a man or woman. Ask any husband or wife, brothers and sisters or any living person.

To forgive yourself, you must first know that you have been forgiven by God. How much ego could a man have if he were not forgiven by God, to think that he could forgive himself? The most healing thing I know is that I am forgiven by God. I like the prayer of the man who prayed, "Lord I have hurt no one today, committed no sin and I thank you for that. I'm going to get out of bed now and things are going to be changing fast." That sounds like a good excuse to sleep more, we sin less.

God Who made us, knowing our frame, is ready and willing to forgive our iniquity.

Psalm 78:38

But he [God], *being* full of compassion, forgave *their* iniquity, and destroyed *them* not: yea, many a time turned he his anger away, and did not stir up all his wrath.

The word "compassion" means to be tender; to have mercy. It comes from an idea of fondness. The word "full" means to have plenty of; to be satiate. God is satiated with compassion. I'm not sure what your mind picture is of that, but I bet it's great. God is fond of us and has plenty of tender mercy toward us. The last anger and wrath I would want to see on my life would be God's. Don't stir up God's pot.

The verse continues, "many a time turned he his anger away." Glory hallelujah for that. God is satiated with love. Love has to be there, and then comes the forgiveness. Little love – little forgiveness. In God's forgiveness, He remits our punishment. How could you feel wanted or needed in a place where you are not forgiven? We could all hang a sign over our front doorway, "Our Home of Forgiving." Forgiveness is like the warmth of heat on a cold day when your teeth are chattering.

There are different administrations in God's Word. We live in what is called the Grace Administration which started on the day of Pentecost as recorded in the book of Acts. We live in the time of grace – not law. We don't have the consequences in our daily living of not keeping the law like those who lived before the time of Christ did. For example, if you don't do this, this will happen; if you do this, this will happen. For instance, the woman taken in adultery would have certainly been stoned to death had Christ not loved her and spoke the new law of love to those accusing her. There were a lot of consequences and penalties for doing or not doing God's Word in the Old Testament. There were many rules, regulations, procedures, laws, orders and precepts to be kept. God has made life so wonderful and great for us. God has given us freedom through Christ Jesus. God's a lot more blessed with how things are now, than He was then. And I'm sure that goes for the rest of us.

We don't recall often enough all that Christ delivered us from. How many laws did the Old Testament believers have to keep? Maybe about as many hairs as we have on our heads. (Just a little humor.) God looks on our hearts. Jesus Christ kept the whole law and never once broke the law. That is the reason we are freed from the law.

We have far more freedom to make mistakes and go against God's Word than the Old Testament people did. I thank God the only law we have today is love God and love your neighbor as yourself. I do my best to do this, but if I lived in the Old Testament I would have been stoned many times over. That's not a figure of speech.

Galatians 5: 1

Stand fast therefore in the liberty wherewith Christ hath made us free, and be not entangled again with the yoke of bondage.

We have the freedom to be who we want, and go where we will. It's the greatest freedom in life and in the world. God's liberty and freedom sets us free. We are no longer held in by the restraints of the law which only Christ could keep and do. We're not enslaved or in bondage. We are a free people. We are free to pursue our own choices, to enjoy our own free will. God has made His Word free to whosoever. It's a free gift to mankind. The free gift of eternal life is the greatest thing God ever did for us and it's available to anyone, compliments of Jesus Christ. My soul may be guilty but my heart is free. We can speak and act with the freedom and boldness God has given us. Christ has made us free.

We have so much to be thankful for. And a *major key* in thankfulness is knowing that we are forgiven. If we do not believe that we are forgiven, what would we have to be thankful for? There is not a better place to live than a place you know you will be often forgiven. There is no place that you would feel more welcome than a place where there is no guilt or condemnation. The world needs forgiveness. Give forgiveness. As God's kids, if we do not show and give our forgiveness to the world, they will never see it or know it. Only God's people can show God's forgiveness.

SPIRITUAL GOODIES
For Forgiveness by Grace

- The pulse of God's heart is in the truth of His Word.

- Christ is the only person who never told a lie about God. Therefore, he's the only one to utter only the truth about God.

- Without God, we would just be a pile of rubble.

- Jesus Christ is the only highway that leads to heaven.

- We find it hard to forgive one person. God's forgiveness is for the whole world. "Come on man! Show the world an example of what your Father is."

- To love God we must know Him. How can you serve God if you don't know Him? How can you know God without knowing His Word?

- You see the needs of others though the eyes of love.

- Forgive with kindness and do it graciously.

- When you find it hard to forgive others the bulk of the reason why is because you have forgotten what God has forgiven you for. Do you think you will need any future forgiveness?

- God can forgive faster than light. Some of the rest of us move like snails.

- Bitterness will rot you from the inside out.

- God said, "Vengeance is mine." You may find yourself in big trouble trying to help God out here.

- To be unforgiving is a weakness you can live without.

- It's a need in the life and soul of every man and woman to desire God's forgiveness.

- If you forget that God continues to forgive you, you will find it hard to forgive others.

- Bitterness and revenge are for the unloving and unkind.

- When we see others "ragging on" someone and we want to help, get in there and fight for them like Christ did. Tell the accusers, "He who is without sin among you, cast the first stone. You reap what you sow, some day it could be you."

- Bitterness kills your heart and eventually your soul.

- How much peace and tranquility do you have when you fail to forgive?

- According to the scriptures, to not forgive is sin plain and clear.

- The heart of the world is hard like rock and as cold as ice.

- There is evilness and seduction that comes with not forgiving.

- There is a power and control that is held over you when you do not forgive.

- Don't be a victim of your own offence, forgive.

- Free yourself from bitterness and malice, forgive.

- Forgiveness is one of the best teachers on how to love and give.

Chapter Fourteen

Prove Me Now

In the last book of the Old Testament, in the Book of Malachi, there is a uniquely beautiful chapter in God's Word that expounds many of God's promises that we will receive, if we give. In this chapter, God asks us to prove him. He does not ask us to prove ourselves, but to prove Him.

God says prove me now and be blessed – blessed because we do what God's Word says which in this context is to give. We only have one life to do God's Word now. If you don't do it now in this life you will never have another chance to do it. The promises that God makes, no business, company or man could ever make or promise. Let's give, prove God and see His promises come to pass. We won't be giving God or the church money for the outreach of His Word in the next life. You will never find a better place to give or spend your money than to give to God. When does God say to prove Him? NOW!

Malachi 3: 6

For I am the LORD, I change not; therefore ye
sons of Jacob are not consumed.

God never changes. He always loves, forgives and has mercy
for his people. That never could be said of man. For the same
reason, because God does not change, just like the sons of Jacob,
we are not consumed. Aren't you thankful that's how God is,
and HE never changes?

Numbers 23:19

God is not a man, that he should lie; neither the
son of man, that he should repent: [to be sorry,
console oneself] hath he said, and shall he not
do it? Or hath he spoken, and shall he not make
it good?

God has never lied, ever. And whatever He said He will do,
He will make it good. God is always good on His promises. We
will never be left wondering.

Numbers 23:20

Behold, I have received commandment to bless:
and he hath blessed; and I cannot reverse it.

God is not like man that He would ever have to say, "I'm
sorry." God's heart always remains constant in blessing His peo-

ple. God wants to bless, and will bless, and He cannot reverse it. Our God is a God worth believing in. Let's work on not just believing in God, but believing God.

Malachi 3:7

Even from the days of your fathers ye are gone
away from mine ordinances, and have not kept
them. Return unto me, and I will return unto
you, saith the LORD of hosts. But ye said,
Wherein shall we return?

Not much has changed for most of God's people regarding this principle. God is endeavoring to soften people's hearts to His Word and will. And God's Word never returns void. God's Word is written for those who will believe, not to the unbeliever or God rejecter.

God's ordinance in this verse refers to the tithe. Tithe means tenth or ten percent. The Old Testament believers were instructed by the law to give ten percent of their money and goods. This ordinance or law was something that God wanted kept. Today, we have been made free from the law. We live in the day of grace – not law. Man is free to choose. The only law we are to live by is the law of love. And, there is no better way to live life. The greatest freedom in life there is, is the walk of love. You can see in God's Word the love people had for God and His people.

The greatest people that walk on this earth are the people that love God and His family.

God wants us to return to Him. Don't be like these people and say, "Wherein shall we return?" God says His people have gone away from giving back to Him. He wills for us to return to Him in our incomes with our hearts first. The Hebrew word for "return" means to come or go back to the same place. At one time they were giving back to God and then they quit. If God's people would return to Him in their finances, which is really a heart issue with God, God will return to them. This allows God to turn and come back. Of course, God turning and coming back is a figure of speech. God has never moved nor changed toward us. It is people who have moved away from God.

I recently saw a billboard by the highway that read, "If God loves us, why is there so much pain and suffering in the world." The question should never be "if God loves us?" The question is do we have confidence and trust toward Him? God has given us His written Word that holds promises, principles and laws that when claimed and operated produce the blessings and benefits God intends for His people. We chose whether we will claim and operate those principles. How many times do we tell our children what is best for them? Do they always listen? Do they sometimes reap to themselves problems and troubles because they ignore our advice? Those of us who have children understand this scenario. Whether a person has faithfully given for many years, has never given anything at all or given very little, if they all lose everything and wind up broke, God is willing to help them all. God is no less willing to help the person who gave nothing or little. God loves us all the same, unconditionally. God has laid out His heart for us in His Word, but to reap the benefits we must believe God and operate the principles.

When we do not give to God, we do not show any appreciation, or credit to God for what we have. What? Are we self-made people and we did it all ourselves? Man pushes God away in his heart. Man brings this on himself. God is ever present wanting our company which is a state of being together and enjoying each other's company. If man can't learn to give God respect and honor in the financial realm, it is not the only area he is short-changing God and himself.

God wants the same state returned – the state of believing Him and relying on Him. He wants His relationship with us restored. Why did God make man? So we would interact and love Him back. God is a lot more about us loving Him than He is about us being all religious, and us seeing how perfect we think we can be. You will never work your way into God's graciousness by being good enough. It's believing that pleases God. God wants us to take Him at His Word. He wants us to give, to function in the body of Christ and be more of a part of the family of God. God wants us to see His heart on why He wants us to give back to him.

God wanted His people back to their former state where He could bless them again. He didn't want His people living in their selfish unbelief. He wanted them to return to Him in their hearts. He wants us to turn from our own way of doing things and return to His way. If we stay away from God, God will stay away from us. He gave us all freedom of will. God doesn't use anybody. Things are to be used, people are to be loved. The unbeliever never gives to God. Do we want to live like the unbeliever in our finances? We are not loved any more or any less by God whether we give or whether we withhold. Giving is about believing God and loving Him.

God has not done away with the principle of giving to Him. God's people go in the wrong direction when they go away from Him, when they withhold from Him. If you're away, you're absent, you are not there doing what you should. God's people had gone away, far away, from just loving Him back, and trusting Him to take care of them. That was the law. We no longer live under the law, so let's not put anybody under it. But remember God's heart does not change. Even though we are no longer required to give by the law of the Old Testament, God wants us to give from the heart and He will bless us abundantly for that giving. He still wants us to give for the outreach of His Word. God's intent is to reach the world with His Word. Those who have been helped by God's Word know how great it is. It is the best and there is nothing better.

In the time of grace with which we live today, God marks no set percentage for giving. There is no exact amount required. However, if you want the blessing, it is up to you to give. We can give with the same hearts the believers did in the Word. Not only do we receive the blessings that they did, but we receive more blessings because we are sons and daughters of God. It is available to walk in the same believing and power as these people did. God put the people in His Word as examples for us to follow. He also recorded some examples of what not to be and do. Giving and sowing incubate financial ideas for abundance. This is in the Word to strengthen and build our believing. It's for our hearts to grow bigger and to learn to trust God more. God just wants some love and respect for all He does for us. Whatever we have, God put that substance in the earth for man to work and change.

Malachi 3:8 & 9

vs 8   Will a man rob God? Yet ye have robbed me. But ye say, Wherein have we robbed thee? In tithes and offerings.

vs 9   Ye are cursed with a curse: for ye have robbed me, even this whole nation.

I know of nowhere after the gospels or in all of the epistles where God says if we don't give of our incomes, we are robbing Him, or we are cursed with a curse. Remember we are not under the law. God does not bring or give sickness to anyone. God does not curse us. We live in the day of grace. Christ died and rose again to pay the price for any and all our sins. That includes all the ones we don't give a hoot about. We will never receive or get consequences from God. If you fail to give there is no suffering for it. Where are the blessings for the withholding of it? Sometimes, though, there are the consequences of our own unbelief. Furthermore, I see no benefits for its neglect either. What I do see is that you won't have room enough to receive the blessings when you do give. As you start to give, God will teach you and your heart will change and soften to Him. Tender-heatedness is a quality that God likes to work with.

Many of God's people refused to limit God in their lives. These people, thousands of years ago, have an effect on this generation. Are our lives going to have a good effect on our children and further generations? Some of us know that if you will change your thinking in this area, God will change your life. The people in Malachi that knew God and loved Him did the will of God. They didn't think it wrong to pray or believe for prosperity. The people who lived the law of tithing then, did not have the fears associated with not giving. God made sure they were taken care of in every area of their lives. We do not have to fear not giving to God today because we are not living under the law. However, if you we do not operate the principle of giving and receiving, we will not have as much believing to receive from God.

No one but Christ could keep and do all the law. We live in grace not law. It's not too late to start giving while you are living. God was reproving Israel for deeds not done. Remember God said, "I change not." He's not going to change His dealings on the conditions stated. God is saying that if we fulfill the condition to His promise, we will receive the blessing. Remember God says, "I lie not." Then if God doesn't lie, He does not lie.

Malachi 3:10

Bring ye all the tithes into the storehouse, that
there may be meat in mine house, and prove me
now herewith, saith the LORD of hosts, if I will
not open you the windows of heaven, and pour
you out a blessing, that *there shall* not *be room*
enough *to receive it.*

The phrase "all the tithes," implies that a part had been withheld. These people were short-changing God. They were "giving" some, but they weren't doing as God's Word instructed them to do. So, they did not receive the benefits because of their own unbelief. No one can hide their heart and intent from God. Be honest with Him or your heart will rat you out.

God's response to that is to ask them to PROVE Him. The word "prove" means to test, to investigate, examine. We use the expression, "prove it." As we might say, "The experiment proved it." If we are to prove God's Word, in the day of grace we live in, we have to practice the principle of giving and receiving. We need to give that part that is being withheld. If you will give a portion faithfully, God will prove His Word and bless you.

To spend your money in just about every place imaginable and not give any to God, well that's just stupid. Some people go to church for the holidays like Easter and Christmas and drop a few dollars into the collection plate. That is not operating the principle of giving and receiving. We are to give of our finances to the church or fellowship where we are being taught God's Word and where our needs are being met. At the end of the Book of Philippians, Paul talks about the principle of giving and receiving. He wants the believers to know that there is a great benefit to them for their giving. And remember, Paul may be doing the writing, but it is God doing the speaking by way of His Word–Paul is the writer, God is the Author.

Philippians 4:15 – 19

vs 15   Now ye Philippians know also, that in the beginning of the gospel, when I departed from Macedonia, no church communicated [shared] with me as concerning giving and receiving, but ye only.

At the time Philippians was written, these believers were the only ones giving to Paul. What's so beautiful about this record is says that they weren't just giving, but that they were also receiving! God's people need to wake up spiritually and see the receiving side of giving. God is not a piker.

> vs 16   For even in Thessalonica ye sent once
> and again unto my necessity.

> vs 17   Not because I desire a gift: but I desire
> fruit that may abound to your account.

I'm writing this LOUD so you can hear it! Paul is telling the believers that he doesn't desire their money, but he desires that they get blessed and have fruit in their lives. Remember it's God's Word. God desires that we have fruit in our lives. God wants us to believe to receive when we give.

> vs 18   But I have all, and abound: I am full,
> having received of Epaphroditus the things *which*
> *were sent* from you, an odour of a sweet smell, a
> sacrifice acceptable, wellpleasing to God.

Who would we want to be more well pleasing to than to God?

> vs 19   But my God shall supply all your need
> according to his riches in glory by Christ Jesus.

God wanted His people to know that He didn't desire the gift, but He desired that fruit would abound to them. He wanted them to know that He would supply ALL their need. So then, when we give, we give to God in our hearts, not to the leaders or ministers of that group. We appreciate the service of the men and women who teach us, but we give to God from the heart. We give to God through the church. Then God will continue to take care of us, our families and all of our needs.

God declares, "I will open the windows of heaven and pour you out a blessing that there shall not be room enough to receive it." The words "pour out" in the older texts read "empty out." God will withhold nothing. He will empty out all His blessings to you. God knows what will bless you more than you do. You can learn to enjoy life right where you're at, no longer hoping for things to change so life will be better.

I know of nothing more than the love of God (*agapeo* in the Greek) that will encourage and motivate a person to sow and reap. How can we serve God with the kind of hearts these people in the Bible did, without loving Him? If we are to love God, we must know God. One of the major principles in my life, of knowing God, is this topic. However well or unwell I know Him, God will be the judge of that someday. I would not know God as I do, if I did not apply the principle of sowing and reaping. I don't have the believing that the men and women in the Word exemplified, but I'm going to keep being on my way. And this principle helps me in so many other areas in my walk. The three areas it helps me most in are prosperity, health and wonderful peace of mind.

God would never ask us to do something or go someplace

where His grace and mercy would not cover or shield us. The primary will of God is to give. Where is there a safer place to live, than in the will of God?

God says He will personally rebuke the devourer for your sake not somebody else's. God will rebuke the devil, the one causing all the poverty and havoc in your life. God can get the devil off your back if you will allow Him. You're not going to do it by yourself. I'm sure God takes great pleasure in kicking the devil in the butt and getting him out of your life, in the financial realm, and other areas as well. This is the rebuke of God the Almighty One.

The devil has plagued God's people too often and for too long. It's not God's fault a person is plagued by debt. It's only your fault if you live there, and continue on living there. God is making a way of escape. People just don't see life in the spiritual realm. You're working hard to get ahead and don't see the devil working hard to see that you don't. He's always trying to hide himself so you don't detect him. The secret to the adversary's success is the secrecy with which he moves. We need to look at life spiritually and not from our senses point of view, which is always distorted and unclear. When you view life by your five senses, you never see what is really going on. In a Christian's finances, the adversary too often escapes and eludes our observation. The devil is called the thief, and far too often he steals our money before we make it. All the money we are making this week is already accounted for and then some. Therefore, we get talked out of doing what we should have done – give. The reason people don't have is because they don't give, therefore they don't receive.

I would say that I don't understand why people don't give, but I haven't always given and applied the principle of giving and receiving. The bottom line is the reason I didn't give was because I didn't take God at His Word. I didn't believe that I would get blessed back for my giving. I guess I just thought I would have less if I gave. Did you notice all the "I's" in that sentence? There is a lot of selfishness in withholding. It is sad to say, but I just must have thought that God was lying to me. I thank God that He woke me up and I didn't have to live my whole life that way.

The devil has stolen from you before you ever acted on what you thought you should do. You had a tremendous idea and the adversary stole your believing. You had a great idea but didn't have the believing to see it through, because you were too afraid of being a loser, or being defeated. Too often, the adversary's methods and means go spiritually unperceived and evade us. He takes what belongs to another and we allow it. He just slips away and we're left wanting and wondering what happened. If you want the one causing the financial problems in your life rebuked, I think you know what to do. Somebody has to rebuke the devil, and that requires you and God. You have to do your part. God is more than willing to do His part. God rebuked satan from Joshua's, Malachi's and many other people's lives in His Word and He can do it for you.

The thinking behind giving and receiving has to be important to you, if you're going to keep doing it as long as you're breathing. In John 13:1 it says that Jesus Christ loved the people unto the end. He walked the Word his entire life. All the way to his last breath, and his last thought, he walked God's Word. Jesus Christ's heart and commitment was to do this his whole life. That is what our mind set should be. Christ set the example to follow. Our heart, commitment, and thinking should be, "I am in this until Christ comes back or I die." You can see that in the hearts and lives of those people who believed Him.

Matthew 22:21b

Render therefore unto Caesar the things that are Caesars: and unto God the things that are Gods.

There is a portion of your income that belongs to God. You need to decide in your heart, between you and God, what that amount is. This is just me, how I handle mine with God. I never have an exact percentage that I give every time. Sometimes it's more, sometimes it's less. I always make sure it's enough that it means something to me. And what I give to God comes off the top first, not second or "here's what's left God." If you love your mom and she had a need, you wouldn't treat her like that. Don't give the scraps and leftovers. No one forces me or makes me give. I give because I want to and I always send it forth with prayer and love. Nor, do I give out of guilt. God is not begging any one for money or calling it a crime if you don't give. God just wants to be loved, and be given some respect. If we can find and see God's heart on why He wants us to give, and we give, it will change our lives. It did mine, and I will witness to it. God is second to none in my finances. I am just glad I can give back to God to help His people. It is of God's own that we give to Him.

Jesus Christ, David, Malachi and many others set this example for us.

I Chronicles 29:9 – 14

vs 9   Then the people rejoiced, for that they offered willingly, because with perfect heart they offered willingly to the LORD: and David the king also rejoiced with great joy.

vs 10   Wherefore David blessed the LORD before all the congregation: and David said, Blessed be thou, LORD God of Israel our father, for ever and ever.

vs 11   Thine, O LORD, is the greatness, and the power, and the glory, and the victory, and the majesty: for all that is in the heaven and in the earth is thine; thine is the kingdom, O LORD, and thou art exalted as head above all.

vs 12   Both riches and honour come of thee,

[and don't ever forget it] and thou reignest over
all; and in thine hand is power and might; and
in thine hand it is to make great, and to give
strength unto all.

vs 13   Now therefore, our God, we thank thee,
and praise thy glorious name.

There is no other principle in our walk whereby we can thank
Him in this way, or praise His glorious name.

vs 14   But who am I, and what is my people,
that we should be able to offer so willingly after
this sort? for all things come of thee, and of
thine own have we given thee.

Verse fourteen is so beautiful and so clear. It is the perfect
heart to have, and you should read it again.

We give to Him because He first gave to us. If we regard giving to God as a weekly or monthly bill, we are missing the heart
of God on why He wants us to give. We have freedom of will and
can distinguish between right and wrong. How could we think it
right to not give. Why have so many become cold, numb and in-
different. God is not guilting us into giving. He is endeavoring to
love us into giving. Guilt often comes around from a voluntary
neglect of a known act. I know we know better. I know we want
to do what's right before God and show our love and thankful-

ness to Him. We have lived with enough guilt and condemnation in our lives. Let's live with guiltlessness. It's like lying, the more you do it, the less it bothers you. There is no punishment for not giving. However, there is no blessing for not giving. I've never found one in the Word.

I don't want your money nor am I asking for it. I thank God that's a responsibility I don't have. We don't run a church or a ministry, so before God scripturally why should we receive it or take it from any one. If you have some work you need done on your home, however, I'll be glad to give you an estimate to do the work and receive my pay that way. I'm in the home improvement business.

In verse ten of Malachi three it says, "there shall not be room enough to receive it." You can put your name in there. You won't have room enough to receive it. I have no problem trying to make extra room for things from God – in my heart, or home.

God said that your barns will be filled with plenty. You will have plenty, you will have an abundance, you will have more than your need met. You will be filled to satisfaction. You will have what you need and want. What does this mean in our everyday lives? It means that my refrigerator is full. My closet is not big enough to hold everything. Your vehicles are in great shape. If you wanted to head out across country tomorrow you could, without the worries of breaking down. Your home has the things in it that bless you. You are blessed to be seen in the clothes you wear. You have MORE than enough to pay your bills, with money left over. You can go where you want to go and buy what you need to buy. When the clerk asks, "Will that be credit or debit?" You will say, "Debit. Hallelujah!" You don't worry about the bills coming in or when the car breaks down. You have the extra money for it, no problem. You have no worries in the material or financial realm. When you give to God, it's the best money given you will ever give. Just ask Malachi, the windows of heaven were open to him by God Himself. Malachi learned how to open the windows of heaven. Let's go to a window and knock on it, with something in the other hand, and live like Malachi, with blessings poured over us.

Malachi 3:11

And I will rebuke the devourer for your sakes,
and he shall not destroy the fruits of your
ground; neither shall your vine cast her fruit before the time in the field, saith the Lord of hosts.

God says a lot in verse eleven. It is absolutely packed with promises. When God said, "The devil shall not destroy the fruits of your ground," what is He saying to His people? The fruits of your ground is whatever business venture you pursue. If you're a farmer, teacher, server, doctor, nurse, real estate agent, cook, hair stylist, grocery store clerk, chemist, plumber, or electrician – whatever you do for a living, God won't allow the adversary to destroy it. He will personally rebuke the lack and need in your life by rebuking the one causing it all. God will not allow the devil to destroy in your future all the blessings He has in store for you. Your prayers and the desires of your heart will come to pass. The dreams you have in your soul will come to fruition. The things we've cherished in our hearts with God, we can now see and live. Our hopes and dreams can now become reality. The fetters and chains of the devil are unbound. This principle unlocks the door to abundance. You will start expecting good things to happen in your life. You will have peacefulness in your heart in the present and your believing will grow for a greater future. You will know in your heart beyond a shadow of a doubt that God has great things coming for you. Your inner heart's desire, that maybe you have only shared with God, will come to pass. This sowing is one of the biggest ways to bring it to pass. This giving is vital in overcoming your doubts so that you can believe God. You have to get the first window open before the others open.

When you don't give you have lower expectations. When you do give, your expectations can take flight. When you don't give to God, it's like you are trying to take off the runway with only one wing. Giving gave the people in the Word a vision of victory for their lives. What these people received in their lives was directly reflected in what they believed and what they gave. Sowing brings a relationship with God that you would otherwise never have.

But, we don't come from the factory wanting to prove what is good, and do the perfect will of God. If you want to develop the habit of blessing God with your income, and receiving blessings back from God, you have to change.

Romans 12:2

And be not conformed to this world: but be ye
transformed by the renewing of your mind, that
ye may prove what is that good, and acceptable,
and perfect, will of God.

As we sin, we continue to develop old man habits. It's the new man that wants to give. When we don't give, we are conformed to the world and live like the people of the world in this area of our lives. The God rejecters and unbelievers don't give to the church for the outreach of God's Word. How many promises do you claim in your sowing and reaping? How many do you know? Filling your mind with the promises of God is how you are going to be able to prove what is that good, and acceptable, and live the perfect will of God.

God wants to do new things for us in our lives – things we have never given Him the opportunity to do because of the lack of our giving and believing. When we fail to give, we miss out on God's best. When we sow, our dreams won't die on the vine. If you want those windows open, give with a heart of love.

Malachi 3:16 & 17

vs 16   Then they that feared [respected] the
LORD spake often one to another: and the
LORD hearkened, and heard *it,* and a book of
remembrance was written before him for them
that feared [respected] the LORD, and that
thought upon his name.

vs 17   And they shall be mine, saith the LORD
of hosts, in that day when I make up my jewels;
and I will spare them, as a man spareth his own
son that serveth him.

Fear is respect. Those that had respect for God spoke often
one to another. I wonder what about. They wanted to fellowship around God's Word. They enjoyed it. If God hearkened
and heard it and there is a book of remembrance written before
Him of those who thought upon His name, they were not talking
about the latest stock. You know what they were talking about.
They were talking about how much God was blessing them. It's a
wonderful thing in life to know other believers who love to spend
time together and do things together and speak about God.

Psalm 133:1

Behold, how good and how pleasant *it is* for
brethren to dwell together in unity.

In verse seventeen, God says that we are His. He is our Father and we are His children. A father is willing to spare nothing to a child who serves Him. We want to be His in a day when He is making jewels. God wants to give us all we can believe to receive. In the older texts, it reads special treasure; a special treasure to appropriate as one's own. Look at God's big heart of giving! And God's heart is the most contagious heart there is. Give to Him and get more of His heart in yours.

God wants to have and keep our company. He wills for us to frequently converse and be associated with Him. Just to be a companion as His friend. He wishes for us to be as though we were accompanying one another. Who could really speak or tell of Jesus Christ's fellowship with God – only the two of them. God made us to converse with Him. God is an individual God. He is personal to each one of us. It means a lot to God for us to keep Him company. And it should mean something to us that He wants our fellowship. We are to enjoy each other's companionship. We are to unite with our Papa for the same purpose. When we go somewhere do we take God with us in our heart and thoughts? When God wants us to go somewhere with Him, do we go? Like when someone is in need that maybe only God knows about, do we go to help? As we grow with God, we then go everywhere together. If you love God the only reason you can, is because He loved you first. Do we desire God's fellowship and that mutual sharing, a Camaraderie that only the spirit of

God within allows? God wants us to share with Him. He wants us to open and pour out our hearts to Him. God's company will be enjoyed more than any other. It is in our best interest to love God above all else.

In our finances, God desires us to agree with Him and do His will. All of us collectively could never out give God. When we trust Him in our financial matters, it brings us closer to God. God does not need our money. God could lay golden eggs the size of Gibraltar all day long. Our Father desires for us to unite with Him in reaching the world with His Word. What we give makes a difference to God, His people and it benefits us. Don't short change God, yourself and the rest of God's family in this life. Furthermore, what you do for God in the here and now will earn you rewards in heaven which you will have the honor of living with for all eternity.

SPIRITUAL GOODIES For Prove Me Now

- God has given it to us straight and clear. He has told us what would happen if we loved stuff, things and the creation more than the Creator. Greed will strip your heart of any love and kindness you have left.

- Everything people have whether they are believers or unbelievers is because of God.

- God's windows are closed. It's giving of our finances that opens those windows. God will personally open His windows and pour you out a blessing that there shall not be room enough to receive it.

- If you want God's inflow, He needs your outflow.

- If you want to do some reaping, you will have to do some sowing.

- Money in and of itself is a blessing to have especially when you're hungry.

- Giving financially to God generates and gives rise to believing.

- When we faithfully practice the principle of giving and receiving, it changes something on the inside of us which then starts to manifest itself on the outside.

- You have to trust God before you will ever believe God.

- Don't allow the world to tell you, "You can't," when every day God is telling you, "You can."

- If you want to experience the power of prayer you will have to spend time doing it.

- People often fear change; it's the fear of the unknown. The thought of not changing would scare me.

- Too many of God's people cannot overcome the enigma of thinking that nothing good will ever happen to them. They ask, "Why do good things only happen to others?" Phrases such as, expect defeat, doomed for life, mundane, routine mediocre life at best are often what people think and believe. It's the Word of God believed that changes people's lives.

- God can soften the hardest of hearts and rein in the stoutest of wills.

- Zacchaeus gave fifty percent of what he made to the poor. The name "Zacchaeus" in Aramaic means pure. He was appropriately named. Christ invited himself to Zacchaeus home and spent time with his family. How blessed would you be.

- The people in the Word of God who gave to God, gave because they believed in the principle and had no regrets nor were they disappointed in their expectations.

- We can learn to give to God with love in our hearts for Him with no ulterior motives.

- Why do people give their money everywhere else and have stinginess in their heart toward God.

- If you are thankful to God on the inside you will express it on the outside to Him.

- Giving back to God is everything God said it to be.

- When you grow to love God there is no part of your life He won't touch or reach.

- I regret in times of need I sometimes worried and became anxious when I should have been peaceful and blessed, continuing to believe God. Time spent worrying is some of the most wasted moments in life.

- How rich we would be if we believed in the wealth of God's love.

Chapter Fifteen
The Prayers of God's People

The heart and love with which the people in the word prayed sets the standard for us to follow. God's Word is His will for our lives. What God says He wants for us in His Word is the will of God for our lives. Which is really a pretty well-kept secret, isn't it? Nobody can say it better than God says it in His Word.

Mark 1:35

And in the morning, rising up a great while
before day, he went out, and departed into a
solitary place, and there prayed.

Christ started his day early in prayer and fellowship with his heavenly Father. He prayed In a solitary place away from all the hustle and bustle of the world. He went to a secluded place, which in this case was the desert. It was just he and God. That was good company; even our moms would let us hang out with these "Guys." Sometimes I think any place destitute of people is a great place to pray. If at all possible get away to a quiet peaceful place where you and your God can be alone. Go to a place where your heart can be at rest and you can be at ease with your thoughts. The most peaceful and quieted my soul has ever been was in times of solitary prayer. On those occasions only the awareness of the presence of God could accomplish the freedom from the disturbance of my heart and my soul. It is refreshing to be free from the alarm and the turbulence that life often brings. The inner quiet seas of the soul that prayer serves on a silver platter can only come from God Himself.

Prayer brings peace of mind and calms the agitated heart. In prayer to God the heart is released from the tumult, disorder and the commotion that the world freely offers and breeds. Prayer has freed me from more internal commotion and emotional warfare in a shorter period of time than anything else. Prayer has healed a lot of us of more than one inner conflict of our souls.

Romans 5:1

Therefore being justified by faith, we have peace
with God through our Lord Jesus Christ:

There is no peace with God outside of Jesus Christ. He is not up there warring against us. God is not condemning us or watching and waiting for us to screw up. Consistent prayer breaks the shackles of sin consciousness. We HAVE peace with God. It is written, we have peace with God through our Lord Jesus Christ. If we only knew how much God really loved us. Even all the Old Testament believers were waiting for Christ's first coming.

Psalm 55:17

Evening, and morning, and at noon, will I pray,
and cry aloud: and he shall hear my voice.

Prayer is a major key of renewing the mind. If you just read the Word and never did what you read, how could you change? We receive the Word, we retain the Word, and we release the Word with boldness. A day in the life of David had some prayer in it. David believed in prayer. He had a life of prayer. It helped him build a close relationship with God. What else did David do twice a day or ten times a day? How big and important is prayer? I can't find anything that David was more faithful to. Who else is it said of in the Word, "he was the apple of God's eye and a man after God's own heart?"

When I first started praying I developed the habit of praying once a day. And I made that one prayer count. It was not a long prayer. I just prayed with as much heart, conviction and trust as I knew how. I also learned that prayer is not exclusive to my own interests without regard for others' needs. And, as time went by and I stayed faithful, not perfect, my trust grew into believing and my prayers began to be answered. As the decades have rolled by, my prayer life has become a wonderful joy. You could take away my home, all my earthly belongings, my Bible, my family, my speech, but no one can take my prayer life away from me. We might not always be able to speak God's word or hear God's Word, but we can always pray. God so valued His relationship with you, that He made it possible for you to fellowship with Him anywhere at any time. Where could you be on this earth and not be able to pray? You could be hanging on a cross and still pray.

Prayer, is of all things, the least selfish act one can do. You can pray for people and it is something they will never know. It can be a life of treasure you are storing up for all eternity. One of the greatest ways to know and fellowship with Him is prayer. We learn what prayer is, why we should pray and what to pray for from God's Word. The hearts and prayers of the people that prayed in the Word were all different. They had different needs, varying one from another. In the same way our needs will be unique to us.

Romans 14:22

Hast thou faith? have it to thyself before God.
Happy is he that condemneth not himself in
that thing which he alloweth.

There is so much variety in the things people prayer for in the Word. What one person may pray and believe God for might be sin for you and vice versa. No one else can judge what people allow in their lives. In truth, only God can be the Judge of the heart. What one person permits may be sin to another. People look at the outside. God looks within. There are some things in our walk with God that are just between you and Him. It is no one else's business. For example what one couple allows of sex in marriage, another couple may think, God forbid. Just a reminder the Word says, "happy is he that condemneth not himself in the thing which he alloweth."

Proverbs 5:19

Let her be as the loving hind and pleasant roe;
let her breasts satisfy thee at all times; and be
thou ravished always with her love.

I didn't write the book. I do see what Solomon liked. Alright you would like the kids to be able to read this book. Happy is he.

Hebrews 4:16

Let us therefore come boldly unto the throne of
grace, that we may obtain mercy, and find grace
to help in time of need.

I know what you're thinking . . . an appropriate verse for me.

We are to go to God boldly and find help in our time of need. We are to empty our hearts out at His throne, so that we get help in our hour of need. We aren't to just go to God, but we are to go BOLDLY to God's throne. The word "boldly" means to go with frankness of speech, out-spokenness, the speaking all one thinks, and fearless candor. When you send your prayer to God's throne, His blessing rides back on your believing.

Colossians 4:2 – 4

vs 2   Continue in prayer, and watch in the same with thanksgiving;

vs 3   Withal praying also for us, that God would open unto us a door of utterance, to speak the mystery of Christ, for which I am also in bonds: [Paul was imprisoned for showing people that God loves them.]

vs 4   That I may make it manifest, as I ought to speak.

Pray for your leaders in the body of Christ. Pray for open doors to speak God's Word and do it with thanksgiving.

I Timothy 2:1 & 2

vs 1   I exhort therefore, that, first of all, sup-
plications, prayers, intercessions, and giving of
thanks, be made for all men;

vs 2   For kings, and for all that are in authority; that we may lead a quiet and peaceable life
in all godliness and honesty.

Pray for the president, vice president and their families and
all those who are in authority, whether you like them or don't
like them. If we don't like them, we better pray the more. The
reason that we pray for them is so we can lead a quiet and peaceable life. This is what praying for the leaders will do for you. The
word, "quiet," means: free from all agitation or free from being
disturbed by others. Praying gives you tranquility and peace.
Prayer causes you to be disposed to peace in your life and heart
regardless of the decisions those in authority make. We are not
going to allow the decisions that others make decide whether
we do, or do not, live more abundantly. Do not allow the world
to dictate that to you.

Philippians 1:9

And this I pray, that your love may abound yet
more and more in knowledge and in all judgment.

This verse is packed with spiritual goodies. This love in Greek is *agape*. It's a love the world does not have. It's a word not used by unbelievers. It's the love of God in a mind that is renewed. This love is a spiritual love that only comes from God. It is a word not found in profane literature. Leaders are to request this for their people. What a heartfelt thing it is to ask when we pray that people will grow to love bigger. In a big nut shell, the sum and substance of this verse is the love of God in its fullest conceivable form. It is love that springs from respect, admiration and devotion to love God. Next to Christ, Paul had one of the biggest hearts of any man that ever lived.

Fear is the biggest form of unbelief there is. Love is fear's biggest enemy. The love of God is by far the master key in overcoming fear. God's love has more substance and essence of believing in it than any other principle in life. God's love is a love you can love yourself with notwithstanding your faults. You don't have to try to love yourself on account of; you can love yourself in spite of. God loves the saint and sinner alike, not because of their actions or inaction. If you never changed a bit for the rest of your life, God loves you just the way you are. God's love for us is unconditional, however we do endear ourselves to God by OUR love and believing.

Truth and love are going to outlast anything. Paul understood this. Imagine being imprisoned for wanting people's love to abound more and more. This love is the only thing that will make a man or woman strong and fearless. Have you ever considered this truth: the love of God never fails? No wonder we failed so much in our old man days. We had no love of God in our hearts. So, if we have areas we are failing in today, we need to ask ourselves if what we are doing is the right and loving thing. Things are to be used, people are to be loved. The world lives it the other way around. Maybe what you are doing is right, and you just need some love to take you over the top. Walking in the love of God is your guarantee of success.

It is also important when looking at prayer to look at what it is not. Jesus Christ handled prayer from that perspective as well.

Matthew 6:1 – 6

vs 1   Take heed that ye do not your alms before men, to be seen of them: otherwise ye have
no reward of your Father which is in heaven.

There is no reward for a heartless prayer, no matter how beautiful the prayer may seem. We cannot have ulterior motives when we pray – you won't even get in God's yard, let alone past His door. To be seen of men, really? If a man or woman prays with a beautiful vocabulary and words with perfect enunciation to be glorified by others for their speech, that is the picture of vain and selfish prayers. We are to glory in God, not in men and that includes your minister or leader. We just do not glory in men!

> vs 2   Therefore when thou doest thine alms,
> do not sound a trumpet before thee, as the
> hypocrites do in the synagogues and in the
> streets, that they may have glory of men. Verily I
> say unto you, They have their reward.

Everyone has heard the term "two faced." In Greek tragedy plays actors held masks up to their faces to show their emotions. One was a sad face and another was a happy face. Neither showed their true face. The Greek word used for these masks is *hupokrites,* those who speak or act from under a mask or guise. This is where we get the word hypocrite. What do we have more of here, stupidity or evil?

> vs 3   But when thou doest alms, let not thy
> left hand know what thy right hand doeth:

> vs 4   That thine alms may be in secret: and thy
> Father which seeth in secret himself shall reward
> thee openly.

> vs 5   And when thou prayest, thou shalt not
> be as the hypocrites are: for they love to pray
> standing in the synagogues and in the corners of
> the streets, that they may be seen of men. Verily
> I say unto you, They have their reward.

vs 6   But thou, when thou prayest, enter into
thy closet, and when thou hast shut thy door, pray
to thy Father which is in secret; and thy Father
which seeth in secret shall reward thee openly.

The word "closet" in this verse is not the kind of a closet we have today where we store our clothes, shoes and accessories. It was a store-chamber, or private room, where treasures were stored. This closet doesn't represent a physical place so much as it represents the special place where you and God commune in private, a place where treasures are shared one with another. The God that created the heavens and the earth wants to spend personal time alone with just you. What a personal and individual God our Father is to us. When God spoke to all the people in the Word, it was Him personally speaking to them. God has communicated with a lot more people than just those recorded in His Word. It is God's heart's desire to have fellowship with everyone. However it's man's free choice whether he wants to have fellowship with God or not. God desires the same communication and fellowship with us as He had with His people in the written Word.

It's clear in the church epistles that God's sons and daughters do not need a representative or substitute to go to God for them. We can go straight to our Father's throne boldly, as He would have it. Christ is also in there fighting for us. What else would our brother be doing.

Romans 8:34

Who is he that condemneth? It is Christ that
died, yea rather, that is risen again, who is even
at the right hand of God, who also maketh inter-
cession for us.

Some things in God's Word we just apprehend and not com-
prehend. Christ is interceding for us still.

vs 7   But when ye pray, use not vain repetitions, as the heathen do: for they think that they
shall be heard for their much speaking.

"Vain repetitions" means praying the same formal prayer
over and over and over and over again. Even you didn't like reading that. You sped read it once. Here's one thing praying like this
will do. A man will always stand condemned in his heart before
God on the field of his own work. Many have a form of godliness, but deny the truth. I rarely picture God as a judge, but
just to build a picture consider this. After hearing prayers of vain
repetitions, can't you just see God with a gavel slamming it on
the bench saying "DENIED?" Or, how about a stamp on a petition in big red letters reading "DENIED?" When we pray from
the heart we want to see the stamp "REQUEST GRANTED."
We're not to be like those who pray with vain repetitions. They
made their choice, and so do we. We do not want to partake in

customary religious forms of worship. Man usually regards appearance only. God observes the heart and motive only.

Hypocrites love to pray. They love to hear themselves speaking. God's ears are deaf to those types of prayers. These prayers are not to the God and Father of our Lord and Savior Jesus Christ. It's the devil's counterfeit to genuine prayer. Those who belong to God and know the value of prayer, love to pray. We will never be bad enough to not pray. And, we will never be too good to stop. Prayer is powerful; it's one of the mightiest things in life. Prayer is a belief that you can make a difference not only in your own life but in the lives of others.

God wants to be loved. That's what He is. Take time out of your busy schedule and pray to Him and let Him know that He is loved by you. We make sure our kids know that we love them, how about taking time for our Father. Many of us even make sure that we spend plenty of time with our pets. Pay the kids no mind when they tell you, you love the dog or cat more than them. God answers prayer when we ante up and believe.

> vs 8   Be not ye therefore like unto them: for
> your Father knoweth what things ye have need
> of, before ye ask him.

God hears the prayers of our hearts. Before we ask God, He knows our need. Sometimes it takes some time before our prayer is answered. There are times when we need to pray for something until it comes to pass. Maybe you have a health problem or a fear you so want to rid yourself of and you haven't been delivered yet. Continue to go to your Father, for He cares for you.

Two people could continue to pray for the same thing. One person's heart is right, the others is not. I don't know who is who or what is what only God really knows the heart of a man. Heaven hears a lot more complaining than it does thanking.

Psalm 34:6

This poor man cried, and the LORD heard him,
and saved him out of all his troubles.

Most of us have been here. Some of us are still there. You don't have to live there, if you don't want to. It was God who saved him out of all his troubles. You cannot have too many troubles to be delivered from.

Psalm 34:17

The righteous cry, and the LORD heareth, and
delivereth them out of all their troubles.

It does not matter who you are or what you have, God delivers and saves us out of all our troubles. Prayer gives you strength and courage for the days ahead. Prayer builds your believing toward God.

Philippians 4:6

Be careful [anxious] for nothing; but in every
thing by prayer and supplication with thanksgiving let your requests be made known unto God.

The words "be careful" is the Greek word *merimnao* which
means, to be anxious. We are not to be OVERLY concerned
about things.

I preformed a wedding for a couple a few of years ago and I
wanted everything to be the very best that it could be for them.
Even though my heart was right, I ended up becoming anxious
and overly concerned about many things. During the ceremony
sweat was running off my face. I allowed my thoughts of care to
become worry instead of a blessing. This year I preformed my
son's wedding ceremony, but this time I made up my mind that
it was going to be fun and I was going to have a good time and
it was a wedding party. It was a joy and I was so blessed to do it.
Welcome to the family Amber.

It is so important to take time and spend it in prayer with
our heavenly Father. He wants to spend time with you. He loves
you and wants you to have peace, joy, trust and believing toward
Him. In order to develop any relationship, you have to spend
time with that person. Prayer is spending time with Him.

SPIRITUAL GOODIES
For the Prayers of God's People

- Prayer is communicating and fellowshipping with our Father.

- Prayer should be viewed as something precious and valuable, like it was for the people in God's Word. Prayer is a priceless thing to learn.

- In prayer most of what God does goes unnoticed. We usually just see the result of God's work.

- If you spend little time in prayer, it's because you believe little in prayer.

- In many of the prayers of women recorded in God's Word, they were simply conversing with God. They were women who knew they had God's attention.

- To pray for others may be the most selfless and the least selfish act in life. Only God knows most of the prayers prayed in life.

- Christ's prayers were him just sharing his heart with his Father. Christ had free and open conversation with God. No one has had the open heartedness and honesty with God like he did.

- Some things are not available from God. You can pray on your knees till the sun comes up and you won't get them. You must know what is available from God and you learn that from His Word.

- I believe in prayer. It's the master key to God's heart and help.

- There are two kinds of prayer: one with your understanding and one in the spirit. Speaking in tongues is prayer in the spirit.

- Prayer is knocking on heaven's door. Believing is the key that opens it.

- Prayer gives you courage and strength for today and the days ahead.

- Prayer glorifies and honors God. No other principle in God's Word is like or equal to the glory that prayer gives to God.

- How many promises are there in God's Word? Prayer brings about the possibility of receiving all of them. How many do you know?

- The prayers of the people in God's Word were just a heart to heart with their Father.

- When you pray for others you will receive blessings.

- The people that love the most, understand the best.

• God made us all to have the need to be wanted and we all want to be needed. We are part of the family of God and God has given us all a function in the body of Christ. There is fulfillment and rest in knowing you are needed and wanted. How empty and sad life is when you have no place where you think you belong.

Chapter Sixteen
More Spiritual Goodies

- Those who miss out on God's love get royally screwed in life.

- You didn't earn eternal life, nor do you receive things from God because you are so good. God blesses you because of your believing. If God's blessings were contingent upon us being good enough, we would all be losers. Eternal rewards are given for works, eternal life is by grace and blessings in the here and now are by believing.

- We are to never change God's Word, God's Word is to change us.

- What's more heavenly than heaven?

- Giving to God in our finances is vital in making the knowledge of God available to many. Thus, it opens the windows of heaven for prosperity to ourselves and others.

- Mommy said to her baby, God bless, you're a mess.

- God loves the evil and the just. That way none of us get missed.

- The people that love the most, fear the least. The people that give the most have the most.

Proverbs 23:7

For as he thinketh in his heart, so is he.

- It's a law that governs every man's life. God said that you will become what you think. Look at the freedom God gave us. What do you want to think and become?

- In delivering people from fear, God is number one in sales. I checked all the way back to Adam and Eve and He's still the only one in the business of deliverance. The sign above His store still reads, "Free Delivery." Thank God Christ paid our debt.

- God's Word must be treated with respect. Its purity and truth must be protected, and its intended message never violated or misrepresented. God's Word is not to be worked carelessly and haphazardly. We are never to use God's Word deceitfully.

- We should not be ashamed when we don't know something about God. We should be ashamed when we say we know when we don't.

- A little pride swallowed never upset the stomach.

- God is eternal. He has no beginning and no end. Always being, always existing.

- It would be a waste of life to allow Christ to remain dormant in you.

- You will never find peace nor fulfillment in the world. It will suck you dry and leave you wanting.

- The world has no answers to life.

- It's believing which brings the seemingly impossible into view.

- You breathe because God allows you to breathe His air.

- Know what the name means before you name your child. Give them something to live up to.

- The adversary works through people, environment, religion and God forbid, you.

- To wait with silent expectation and submission is an important key in hearing from God.

- It's light that dispels darkness. The darker the night the brighter the light. Let your light shine before men.

Bibliography

The Analytical Greek Lexicon Revised, Grand Rapids, MI: Zondervan
  Publishing House, 1978

*The Baker Encyclopedia of Bible People: A Comprehensive Who's Who from
  Aaron to Zurishaddai*, Grand Rapids, MI: Baker Books, 2006

Berry, George Ricker, PH.D., *The Interlinear Literal Translation of The Greek
  New Testament*, Grand Rapids, MI: Zondervan, 1976

Brenton, Sir Lancelot C.L., *The Septuagint with Apocrypha: Greek and
  English*, Grand Rapids, MI: Zondervan Publishing House, 1851

Brown, F., S. Driver, and C. Briggs, *The Brown-Driver-Briggs Hebrew and
  English Lexicon*, Peabody, MA: Hendrickson Publishers, 1906

Bullinger, E.W., *The Campanion Bible, The Authorized Version of 1611*,
  Grand Rapids, MI: Kregel Publications, 1922

Bullinger, E.W., *A Critical Lexicon and Concordance to the English and Greek
  New Testament*, Grand Rapids, MI: Kregel Publications, 1908

Bullinger, E.W., D.D., *Figures of Speech Used in the Bible*, Grand Rapids, MI:
  Baker Book House, 1898

The Complete Word Study: New Testament with Parallel Greek, Chattanooga,
  TN: AMG Publishers, 1992

Expository Dictionary of Bible Words, Peabody, MA: Hendrickson
  Publishers, 2005

Harris, R. Laird, Gleason L. Archer, Jr., Bruce K. Waltke, *Theological Wordbook of the Old Testament*, Chicago, IL: The Moody Bible Institute, 1980

Holy Bible From the Ancient Greek Text: George M. Lamsa's Translations From the Aramaic of the Peshitta, New York, NY: HarperSanFrancisco, 1957

The Holy Bible: Translated From the Latin Vulgate, London, United Kingdom: Baronius Press Limited, 2003

Morrish, George, *A Concordance of the Septuagint*, Grand Rapids, MI: Zondervan Publishing House, 1887

Mounce, William D., *Basics of Biblical Greek*, Grand Rapids, MI: Zondervan, 1993

New Bible Dictionary, 2nd ed., Wheaton IL: Tyndale House Publishers, 1982

Oxford Bible Atlas, :Oxford University Press, 1974

Pillai, Bishop K.C., D.D.,*Light Through an Eastern Window*, New York, NY: Robert Speller & Sons, 1963

Strong, James, LL.D., S.T.D., *The New Strong's Exhaustive Concordance of the Bible*, Nashville, TN: Thomas Nelson Publishers, 1995

Thayer, J.H., *The New Thayer's Greek-English Lexicon of the New Testament*, N.p.: Christian Copyrights, Inc., 1981

Theological Dictionary of the New Testament, Grand Rapids, MI: WM. B. Eerdmans Publishing Co., 1971

Vine, W.E., Unger, Merrill F., White, William, Jr., *Vine's Complete Expository Dictionary of Old and New Testament Words*, Nashville, TN: Thomas Nelson Publishers, 1996

Webster's New World Dictionary and Thesaurus, 2nd ed., Cleveland, OH: Wiley Publishing, Inc., 2002

Wigram, George V., *The Englishman's Greek Concordance of the New Testament*, Peabody, MA: Hendrickson Publishers, 1903

Wigram, George V., *The Englishman's Hebrew Concordance of the Old Testament*, Peabody, MA: Hendrickson Publishers, 1874

Wigram, George V., and Ralph D. Winter, *The Word Study Concordance: A Modern, Improved, and Enlarged Version of both The Englishman's Greek Concordance and The New Englishman's Greek*, Wheaton, IL: Tyndale House Publishers, 1972

Wilson, William, *Old Testament Word Studies*, Grand Rapids, MI: Kregel Publications, 1978

Winter, Ralph D. and Roberta H., *The Word Study New Testament*, Wheaton, IL: Tyndale House Publishers, 1978

Young, Robert, LL.D., *Analytical Concordance to the Bible*, Grand Rapids, MI: WM. B. Eerdmans Publishing Co., 1970

CPSIA information can be obtained at www.ICGtesting.com
Printed in the USA
LVOW121105040512

280335LV00004B/1/P